ANTOINE'S RESTAURANT COOKBOOK

Antoine's Restaurant

Since 1840

COOKBOOK

A collection of the original recipes from
New Orleans' oldest and most famous restaurant
by Roy F. Guste, Jr.
Fifth-Generation Proprietor

W. W. Norton & Company
New York • London

Copyright © 1980 by Roy F. Guste, Jr.

Published simultaneously in Canada by George J. McLeod Limited, Toronto. Printed in the United States of America.

All Rights Reserved

Library of Congress Cataloging in Publication Data

Guste, Roy F
  Antoine's Restaurant, since 1840, cookbook.

  Includes index.
  1. Cookery, American—Louisiana. 2. Antoine's
Restaurant. I. Antoine's Restaurant. II. Title.
TX715.G985 1979   641.5   80–15029
ISBN 0-393-02666-3

, 1 2 3 4 5 6 7 8 9 0

For Mimi

Contents

HORS D'OEUVRES
Appetizers

POTAGES
Soups

POISSONS
Fish and Seafood

OEUFS
Eggs and Omelettes

VOLAILLE
Poultry

VIANDES
Meats

SAUCES

Sauces (continued)

LEGUMES
Vegetables

SALADES
Salads

Salads (continued)

DESSERTS
Desserts

BOISSONS
Drinks

LIST OF ILLUSTRATIONS

Merryl Tanner, a veteran in the New Orleans art world, has captured the spirit of Antoine's kitchen in her expressive paintings.

Coleman Heriard's works represent his first endeavor in the commercial art field. A self-taught artist, he has beautifully illustrated the products used in the preparation of Antoine's cuisine.

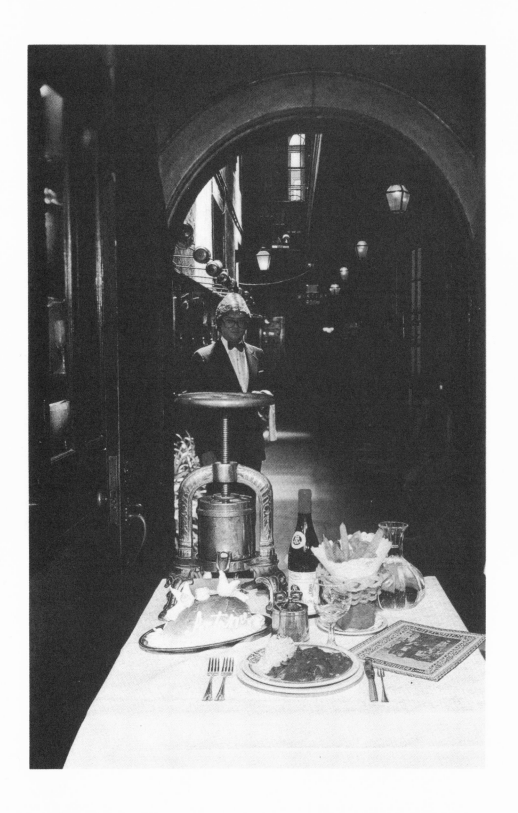

Introduction

It was immediately after my eighteenth birthday that I began working at Antoine's. It had always been assumed by all members of the family, including myself, that I was going to follow my father's footsteps and become an attorney. My reason for working at the restaurant was merely to make some spending money during my college years.

From my first night's work, however, a strong interest began to develop within me, an interest in the restaurant and a concern for the future of Antoine's. As time passed I moved from one area of the restaurant to the next, until I was familiar with all sides of the operation. I took time out to go to France to study cuisine. I met France's greatest restaurateurs and familiarized myself with their restaurants and their food.

At Antoine's I worked to update and improve all facets of the restaurant, taking great care to do so without any apparent change, other than improvement, from the viewpoint of our clientele.

The family members watched and judged my every move. In December of 1975, the Alciatore-Guste family made an extremely bold move: they named me, at twenty-four years of age, the proprietor of Antoine's.

I have been criticized and complimented for my management of Antoine's but can say, with all sincerity, that everything I have done or have attempted to do has been for the betterment of all concerned, customers, employees and owners alike.

This book is a statement of my own feelings, gained from my own experience and that of the greatest chefs and restaurateurs with whom I have had the good fortune to spend time. This statement is that there is no value to "secrets" in cuisine.

Most likely in past times there *was* some value in protecting one's own ideas and creations, but today, the value lies in quality of production. There are very few restaurants today that strive to attain the same quality that we work unceasingly to retain. There are innumerable problems involved in doing so and little in return by comparison.

It is also my experience that those persons most interested in producing our dishes themselves are also our most frequent visitors. And these visitors come not just for the food but for the total experience of dining at Antoine's: the simple, but elegant and comfortable atmosphere, the relationship of clients to waiters, the generations of families, customers and workers, and owners that have all contributed to the continued existence and operation of Antoine's.

Oysters Rockefeller! — the one important recipe that I have not included in this volume. I have not omitted this to retain the secret of the original recipe created by Great-grandfather Jules. I quite simply feel that it is not mine to give. It is as though it is a part of the physical structure which cannot be removed. And it is most definitely a part of the magic that still exists, more strongly than ever, in the soul of Antoine's.

Roy F. Guste, Jr.

An old print from Harper's believed to be the dining room of Antoine's at the original location in the 600 block of Rue St. Louis.

L'HISTOIRE

The History of Antoine's

In April of 1840 a young man, 16 years old, opened the doors to a small *pension* on Rue St. Louis. This man was my great-great-grandfather Antoine Alciatore.

Antoine grew up in Marseilles, France; his father, Joseph Alciatore, was a wool merchant there. At a very young age Antoine was apprenticed to the owner of the Hotel de Noailles and began working in the kitchen. During his apprenticeship he became a qualified chef and even learned the secret of Pommes de Terre Soufflees from the great chef Collinet.

Antoine became restless in Marseilles and soon decided to seek his fortune in the New World. He boarded a ship to the United States (to New York), taking with him all the money that he had saved and whatever his parents could spare.

On the boat young Alciatore met and became friendly with a young Alsatian girl, Julie Freyss, who was coming to the United States with her parents to settle in New York. Julie and Antoine became very close. He told her that he was going to New Orleans to find his fortune, and that as soon as he had established himself he would send for her and they would be married.

Once in New Orleans, young Antoine found himself in the environment he had longed for, and again in a city that spoke his native tongue.

He first found employment in the St. Charles Hotel, which was then just a year old, but was soon lured into the heart of the city, to the first municipality, which we now call the "Vieux Carre." There he rented a building at 50 St. Louis Street and opened a small *pension* or boarding house. This is now the 600 block of St. Louis Street and is occupied by the Old Civil Court House.

From here the fame of Antoine's began to spread with travelers and the citizenry of New Orleans alike. Antoine had brought his knowledge of *La Cuisine Francaise, La Cuisine Provencal* and his own ability to create and adapt the products of the area for the people of the area.

Antoine Alciatore

It was five years after his arrival in New Orleans that Antoine sent for Julie. She traveled to New Orleans and they were married as promised. Together they worked in the small *pension*, which was now becoming more restaurant than boarding house, and soon outgrew this location. In 1860 they moved the business to a larger building, the Lacoul residence, located at what is now 714 St. Peter Street.

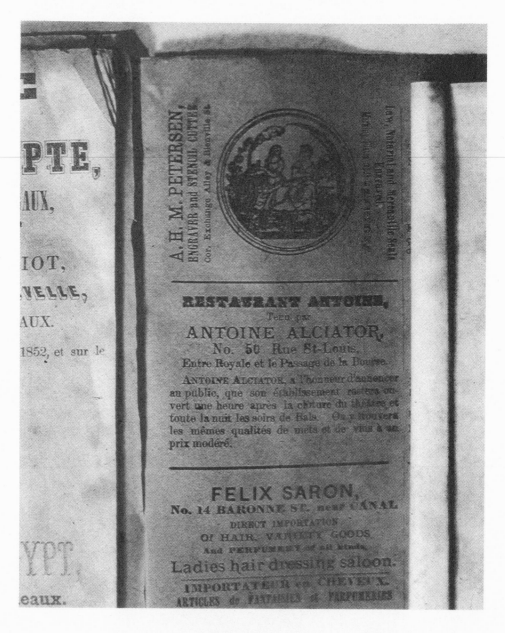

Above: An advertisement from the opera program, February 1852.
"Antoine Aliciatore has the honor to announce to the public that his establishment will remain open one hour after the closing of the theatre, and all night the evening of the (Carnival) Balls. One will find the same quality of food and wine at a more moderate price."

Right: Antoine Alciatore and his first five sons, including Jules, the next-to-youngest in this photograph, taken about 1870.

By 1868 Julie and Antoine had seven children; both family and business had outgrown their St. Peter Street residence. Antoine had for some time been planning to build his own place and had acquired a piece of land from the Miltenberger family. Antoine and Julie built themselves a building grand enough for a larger restaurant, for the family residence, and for some guest rooms for friends and discerning travelers. One of the guests who, with his wife and children, would stay at Antoine's was Pierre Bienvenu Roy, a planter from Youngsville in the parish of Lafayette, Louisiana.

In early 1877, Antoine was told by his physician that he was dying of tuberculosis. He arranged his affairs and informed his wife and children that he wanted to die and be buried in Marseilles. "I do not wish you to accompany me, for it would only prolong any sorrow you might feel, were you to watch me fail, day by day, as I neared the grave. Just think of me as though I had already died, for when we part, as I take the boat for Marseilles, we will not meet again on earth." Within three months of his arrival in Marseilles, Antoine died in his mother's home at the age of 52.

The main dining room at Antoine's present address. One of 14 dining rooms of many styles and sizes.

Julie Freyss Alciatore
(Mme Antoine)

Mme Antoine carried on the operation after her husband's death. It was her son Jules, who was only eleven years old, who began to show the most intense interest in the restaurant. For the next six years Mme Antoine took young Jules as an apprentice and taught him all she had to teach. At seventeen Jules was sent abroad to France to work in some of the greatest kitchens in Strasbourg, Paris and Marseilles. He even went for a while to London.

After four years abroad, Jules returned to New Orleans, but his mother was still not ready to give him full control of the restaurant. She wanted him to work for awhile as manager of another restaurant, to prove he was ready. Jules became the chef of the famous Pickwick Club in New Orleans. In 1887 his mother asked him to take over the operation of Antoine's.

Some time later, Pierre Bienvenu Roy came to New Orleans to do some business here and to stay with his dear friend Mme Antoine. He brought with him his daughter Althea, who won the attention of Jules. Some weeks later Jules was off to Lafayette, to the plantation of the Roys, to meet Althea's entire family and woo her into becoming his wife.

Jules was successful in his mission and soon they were married.

It was not long before Althea gave birth to a daughter, Marie Louise, then a son, Jules, and then another son, Roy.

Jules was a master of his art and brought the name of Antoine's to international fame. He was responsible for a major part in the growth of the restaurant. He created many dishes, the most famous being Oysters Rockefeller.

Right: Jules Alciatore, 1865-1934
Below: The children of Antoine and Julie
Alciatore.

The third Jules found his passion not in cuisine, but rather in romance languages and became a distinguished professor of language. It was Roy who was to carry on the house of Antoine, and he set to work learning the business under his father's careful tutelage.

In 1923, father Jules took Roy to France and to the great kitchens there, so that Roy might observe and remember all that he saw and tasted. Jules gradually handed over the responsibilities of the operation to Roy, so that in 1934, when Jules died, there was an easy transition of proprietorship from father to son.

Right: The Alciatore family, taken in the courtyard of Antoine's in 1912. Madame Antoine, center, was 91 years old. Jules is seated on the left, his son, Roy Alciatore, is third from right, just behind his grandmother.

Below: The Alciatore family and restaurant staff in front of Antoine's in 1885. Madame Antoine is the woman farthest right and Jules is fourth from the left.

Roy Alciatore,
1902-1972

Roy continued the operation, expanding and improving through the years. He added the 1840 Room, a small private room designed to honor the year Antoine's was founded, and the Rex Room, decorated to honor the society and past kings of the Krewe of Rex of Mardi Gras.

Roy also created and added many dishes to the menu such as Pigeonneaux Royaux Sauce Paradis.

Roy Alciatore ran the restaurant from 1934 until the middle sixties, when his nephews Roy and Billy Guste, Jr., sons of his sister (now Marie Louise Alciatore Guste) came in to help him modernize accounting procedures. These nephews are both lawyers and handled all the legal work for Antoine's. When Roy Alciatore died in 1972, Roy and Billy Guste took over the proprietorship of the business for the family.

Right and next page: Antoine's Menu, used from about 1910 to 1940.

16

"ALLONS CHEZ ANTOINE."

ANTOINE'S
ESTABLISHED 1840

MENU

$1.00 PER PERSON MINIMUM

ANTOINE'S SPECIAL

Huitres en coquille à la Rockefeller (Our creation), .60

Pommes, Soufflée, .40   Canapé Caviar, .75

Canapé d'Anchois, .75

Crevette Cocktail, .50   Crabmeat Cocktail, .50

Canapé St. Antoine, .50   Canapé Balthazar, .60

Canapé Rothschild, .75   Côtelettes d'Agneau Maison d'Or, 1.25

Champignons Frais sur Toste, .75

—— Potages ——

Gumbo Créole, .35   Bisque d'Ecrevisses, .25

Potage Tortue, .25   Consommé à la Nilson, .25

—— Poisson ——

Truite Meuniére, .75   Filet de Sole Florentine, .75

Filet de Sole à la Marguéry, .90   Pompano en Papillotte, .90

Crevettes Marinière, .75   Casseburgau Hollandaise, .90

Pompano Pontchartrain, 1.25   Filet de Sole Colbert, .90

Terrapine à la St. Antoine, 1.00   Marquereau Grillé, .75

Huitre Bourguignonne, .60

Poisson Royal Albert, .90   Busters Grillé, 1.00

Pompano Grillé, 1.00   Soft Shell Crabs, 1.00

—— Oeufs ——

Omelette Nature, .40   Oeuf Coolidge, .75

Omelette Espagnole, .60   Oeuf Sardou, .60

Oeuf Balthazar, .60   (2) Oeufs St. Denis, .75

Oeuf Florentine, .60   Oeuf Coquelin, .60

Oeufs aux Tomate à la St. Antoine, .50

—— Releve ——

Paté de Foi Gras à la Gelée (Imported from Strasbourg), 1.00

—— Entrees ——

Poulet Parisienne, 1.25   Poulet Bordelaise, 1.25

Poulet Cocotte, 1.25   Poulet à la Creole, 1.25

Poulet Champignon Frais, 1.50   Poulet Rochambeau, 1.25

Entrees — Continued

Filet de Boeuf Robespierre (En Casserole), 2.50
(2) Côtelettes d'Agneau Grillées, .90
Côtelettes d'Agneau Maison d'Or, 1.25　　　Poulet Grillé, 1.00
Poulet Crapaudine, 1.25　　　Dinde Rochambeau, 1.50
Côtelettes d'Agneau Parisienne, 1.25　Riz de Veau Financiere, .75
Filet de Boeuf Nature, 1.50
(avec sauce), 1.75　　(avec Champignons Frais), 2.00
Entrecôte Grillé Nature, 1.25
(avec sauce), 1.50　　(avec Champignons Frais), 1.75
Filet de Boeuf Marchand de Vin, 1.75
Filet Mignon, 1.75　　　　　　　Tournedos Medicis, 1.50
Côtelettes d'Agneau Champignons Frais, 1.50
Carré d'Agneau Boulangère, 1.25

—— Salades ——

Coeur de Palmier, .75　　　　　Fond d'Artichaut Bayard, .60
Salade Mirabeau, .40　　　Salade aux Pointe d'Asperges, .40
Laitue et Roquefort, .50　　　　Salade Antoine Special, .40
Tomate Frappée à la Jules Caesar, .40

—— Dessert ——

Gâteau Moka, .25　　　　　Crême à la Vanille, .20
Méirngue Glacée, .25　　Omelette Historiée à la Jules Caesar, 1.50

—— Fromage ——

Roquefort, .30　　　　　　　　Gruyere, .30
Camembert, .30

—— Cafe ——

Grand Café, .15　　　Café au Lait, .15　　　Demi-tasse, .10
White Rock, .60 and .30　　　Budweiser, .25
Ginger Ale, .30　　　　　　　Jax, .20
Cigars　　　　　　　Cigarettes

ROY L. ALCIATORE, Proprietor
717 ST. LOUIS STREET

Right and next page: The present menu, created when
the restaurant celebrated its one hundredth anniversary
in 1940 and changed very little since then.

In 1969 Roy Guste, Jr., son of Roy Guste, graduated from high school, began
college and started to work part time at Antoine's. Roy, Jr., was headed toward a
degree in law, like his father and his grandfather, but became intrigued by Antoine's
and was soon off to France to learn the language and cuisine. After a stay of about a
year and a half, combining study in the cooking schools of Paris and work tours in
great restaurants, and becoming generally familiar with the chefs and owners of the
greatest houses of France, young Roy returned to New Orleans to dedicate himself
to the continuation of the House of Antoine.

In December of 1975, Roy Guste, Jr., a mere 24 years old, was officially named
proprietor of Antoine's and given the reins of the operation by the family owners.

Roy F. Guste, Jr.

ANTOINES

1840 CENTENNIAL 1940

Restaurant Antoine

Fondé En 1840

Le service chez Antoine exclusivement à la carte

Minimum 6.00 par personne

NOUS RECOMMANDONS

Huîtres en coquille à la Rockefeller (notre création) 4.25

Huîtres nature 3.75	Crevettes à la Richman 4.00	Canapé St. Antoine 4.25
Huîtres Thermidor 4.25	Crevettes cardinal 4.00	Ecrevisses sous cloche (de saison)
Huîtres Bienville 4.25	Crevettes rémoulade 4.25	Ecrevisses à la marinière (de saison)
Huîtres à la Ellis 4.25	Avocat crevette Garibaldi 4.50	Ecrevisses cardinal (de saison) 4.
Huîtres à la Foch 4.25	Cocktail aux crevettes 4.00	Champignons sur toste 3.25
Huîtres bonne femme 4.25	Tomate frappée à la Jules César 4.00	Champignons sous cloche 4.00
Huîtres Bourguignonne 4.25	Chair de crabes ravigote 4.40	Anchois sur canapé 3.00
Canapé Balthazar 4.25	Chair de crabes St. Pierre 4.25	Canapé Rothschild 3.75
Les escargots à la Bourguignonne 4.50	Chair de crabes au gratin 4.25	Caviar sur canapé 5.00
Les escargots à la Bordelaise 4.50	Cocktail à la chair de crabes 4.40	Foie gras de Strasbourg à la gelée 5
Crevettes à la marinière 4.00	Avocat à la chair de crabes Garibaldi 4.40	Les hors-d'oeuvre froids 4.40

POTAGES

Gombo créole 2.50	Potage tortue au sherry 2.50
Bisque d'écrevisses cardinal 2.75	
Consommé chaud au vermicelle 2.35	Consommé froid en tasse 2.35
Vichyssoise. 2.35	Bisque de crevettes 2.75 Soupe à l'oignon gratinée 2.50

POISSONS

Filet de truite meunière 8.50	*Pompano* en papillote 11.50
Filet de truite à la Marguery 8.75	*Pompano* amandine 10.00
Filet de truite au vin blanc 8.75	Filet de flet Colbert 9.00
Filet de truite amandine 8.75	Crevettes à la créole 8.25
Filet de truite florentine 8.75	Salade de crevettes 8.50
Pompano grillé 9.50	Langouste grillée 15.00
Pompano à la marinière 10.00	Langouste sautée 15.00
Pompano Pontchartrain 11.00	Langouste Thermidor 15.00
Bouillabaisse à la Marseillaise (commander d'avance) 13.50	
Crabes mous grillés 8.75	Chair de crabes marinière 9.00
Crabes mous frits 8.75	Chair de crabes ravigote 9.50
Crabes mous amandine 9.00	Salade de chair de crabes 9.50
Chair de crabes sautée champignons 9.75	Chair de crabes au gratin 9.00

OEUFS

Oeufs Benedict 5.75	Omelette nature 4.75
Oeufs Sardou 5.75	Omelette au fromage 5.00
Oeufs St. Denis 5.75	Omelette aux crevettes 6.00
Oeufs à la florentine 5.75	Omelette à la chair de crabes 6.00
Oeufs aux tomates St. Antoine 5.75	Omelette espagnole 5.75

ENTREES

Poulet aux champignons 8.75	Poulet sauce Rochambeau 9.50
Poulet sauté demi-bordelaise 8.75	Poulet à la parisienne 9.25
Poulet à la créole 9.00	Poulet bonne femme (40 minutes) 9.25
Poulet au vin rouge 9.25	Pigeonneaux Paradis (40 minutes) 9.75

Antoine's

Depuis Plus De 100 Ans.

Restaurant Antoine

Fondé En 1840

AVIS AU PUBLIC

*Faire de la bonne cuisine demande un certain temps. Si on vous fait attendre,
c'est pour mieux vous servir, et vous plaire.*

ENTREES (SUITE)

Côtelettes d'agneau grillées 15.25

Noisettes d'agneau Maison d'Or 16.25

Ris de veau à la financière 9.25

Entrecôte nature 13.50

Tips de filet en brochette Médicis 10.00

Tournedos nature 11.25

Filet de boeuf nature 14.50

Châteaubriand (pour deux (2)—30 minutes) 30.75

SAUCES

Alciatore 1.80   Marchand de vin 1.80   Béarnaise 1.80   Médicis 1.80

Maison d'Or 1.80   Financière 1.80   Robespierre 1.80

Champignons 1.80   demi-bordelaise 1.80

LEGUMES

Epinards sauce crème 2.00

Petits pois à la française 2.00

Chou-fleur au beurre 2.00

Chou-fleur au gratin 2.00

Carottes au beurre 2.00

Broccoli sauce hollandaise (de saison) 2.25

Asperges au beurre (de saison) 2.25

Haricots verts au beurre 2.00

Pommes de terre au gratin 2.00

Pommes de terre brabant 2.00

Pommes de terre soufflées (pour deux 2) 3.50

SALADES

Salade Antoine 2.00

Salade de laitue et tomates 2.00

Salade de laitue au roquefort 2.25

Salade d'anchois 2.25

Salade de légumes 2.25

Avocat à la vinaigrette 2.00

Avocat évantail 2.25

Salade Mirabeau 2.25

Fonds d'artichauts Bayard 2.50

Salade de coeur de palmier 2.50

Salade aux pointes d'asperges 2.00

FROMAGES

L'Assiette de fromages d'aujourd'hui 3.50

Roquefort

Camembert

Brie

Suisse

Port Salut

DESSERTS

Crème glacée — vanille, chocolat, fraises 1.50

Sorbet — orange, citron-vert, ananas 1.50

Méringue glacée sauce chocolat 2.00

Crème glacée aux fraises 2.00

Cerises jubilée 3.75

Pêche Melba 2.75

Patisserie 2.00

Mousse au chocolat 2.00

Crème renversée au caramel 2.00

Crêpes Suzette 3.75

Gâteau moka 2.00

Fraises au kirsch 2.75

Omelette Alaska Antoine (pour deux (2)—commander au commencement du repas) 7.00

CAFE ET THE

Café .75   Thé .75   Thé glacé .75

Café au lait .75   Café brûlot diabolique 3.00   Demi-tasse .75

EAUX MINERALES—BIERES—CIGARES—CIGARETTES

Cigarettes   Bière locale   Bière importée   Cigares

Vichy   Perrier   Evian

Roy F. Guste, Jr., Propriétaire
Cinquième Génération

713-717 Rue St. Louis   Nouvelle Orléans, Louisiane

The most famous New Orleans specialty is perhaps the oyster — Louisiana's are often considered the best and the styles of preparation, invented at Antoine's, are on menus all over the world. Michael Regua, assistant day chef, has been at Antoine's for almost 10 years.

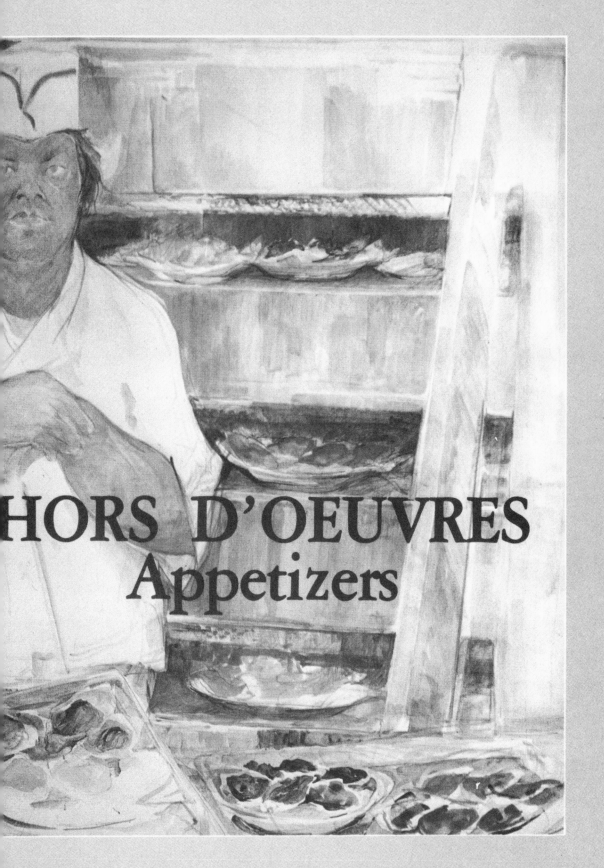

HORS D'OEUVRES
Appetizers

Appetizers have always been one of the strongest areas of our
entire menu. Many of our most interesting and most famous dishes
are included in this section. They are of such great number that it is
not uncommon for diners to make complete meals from four or five
courses of appetizers.

HUITRES NATURE
Raw Oysters

Even considering the innumerable preparations that Antoine's and New Orleans have for oysters, I would venture to say that most of the oysters consumed in New Orleans are consumed raw.

I remember an article written a few years ago by a well-known French restaurant critic who praised Antoine's for its sauces and dishes and everything that came out of the kitchen, except oysters. After all the fuss about the good food his final statement was that Antoine's only downfall was the fact that we cooked oysters. This particular fellow was probably, in fact, voicing the opinion of the entire country of France, where no one ever cooks an oyster, the point being that the oyster in itself is perfection and should not be changed. It's most amusing to me to see that within the past few years dishes have appeared on the menus of the great restaurants of France which are cooked oysters with sauces resembling ours.

It is certainly refreshing for me to see the Parisians stealing something from the New Orleanians rather than the New Orleanians stealing from the Parisians. In any case, we fortunate people in New Orleans still have our oysters raw as often as we like and cooked as often as we like. The great abundance of our oysters makes all good preparations quite welcome.

RAW OYSTERS

3 dozen raw oysters on the half shell
6 pie pans filled with crushed ice
1½ cups Cocktail Sauce, page 117
3 lemons, halved

Arrange six oysters on the half shell on each of the ice-filled pie plates. Fill a two-ounce glass container with Cocktail Sauce and place in the middle of each of the six pans of oysters.

Serve garnished with ½ lemon.

Serves 6.

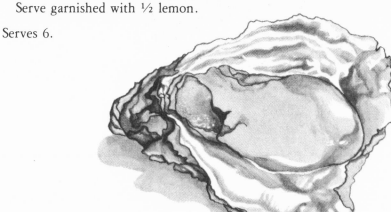

HUITRES THERMIDOR
Oysters Thermidor

Thermidor is the name given to the revolution in France which brought with it the fall of Robespierre and his followers in the summer of 1794. This short revolution marked the end of the reign of terror in an apparently very bloody scene. Again, Jules Alciatore brought in a bit of history of which he was reminded by the blood red sauce called Thermidore.

OYSTERS THERMIDOR

3 dozen oysters on the half shell
3 cups Cocktail Sauce, page 117
3 dozen two-inch pieces bacon

Place the oysters in a preheated 400 °F oven and bake until their edges begin to curl. Remove from oven and cover with Cocktail Sauce. Top each oyster with a piece of bacon and return to the oven. Cook for 5-7 minutes more.

Serves 6.

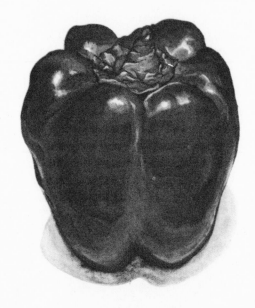

HUITRES BIENVILLE
Oysters Bienville

Jean Baptiste LeMoyne, Sieur de Bienville, an early colonial governor of Louisiana was born in Montreal, Canada, in 1680 and died in Paris in 1768. He was the eighth of eleven sons of Charles LeMoyne. In 1698, Pierre LeMoyne, Sieur d'Iberville, the brother of Bienville, set out to begin a colony at the mouth of the Mississippi. But is wasn't until 1718 that Bienville, with the help of eighty French exiles, cleared some wilderness near the mouth of the river and established La Nouvelle Orleans.

From time to time we may forget that Bienville helped found the city of New Orleans, but we will never forget the oysters named in his honor.

OYSTERS BIENVILLE

3 dozen raw oysters on the half shell
6 pie pans filled with rock salt
5 cups Bienville Sauce

Place 6 raw oysters on the half shell on each of the six pie pans filled with rock salt. Cover each oyster with Bienville Sauce and bake in a 400 °F oven for 10 minutes or so until the oysters and sauce are very hot and begin to brown on top. Serve immediately.

The purpose of the rock salt is to retain heat even after the oysters are brought to the table. Be careful that you don't let the salt get into the oyster shells or into the Bienville Sauce.

BIENVILLE SAUCE

½ stick butter
1½ cups minced bell pepper
1 cup minced green onion
2 cloves garlic, minced
½ cup white wine

½ cup chopped pimento
2 cups Bechamel Sauce, page 123
⅔ cup ground American cheese
½ cup breadcrumbs
salt and ground white pepper

Melt the butter and saute the bell pepper, green onions and garlic until they are limp. Add the white wine and bring to a boil. Now add the pimento, the Bechamel Sauce, the grated cheese and breadcrumbs. Add salt and pepper to taste and simmer for 20 minutes or until the sauce is very thick.

Makes 5 cups.

NOTE: One of our old chefs of forty-eight years named Pete Michel, who has since passed away, told me one day that he and Roy Alciatore invented this dish approximately 40 years ago.

HUITRES A LA ELLIS
Oysters Ellis

A prominent New Orleanian, Crawford Ellis, was honored by his friend Jules Alciatore with the creation of this dish. This preparation has been one of the favorites of local clientele since its inception.

OYSTERS ELLIS

3 dozen oysters in their water	1 teaspoon sugar
3 tablespoons butter	2 tablespoons vinegar
¾ cup finely chopped onions	¼ teaspoon anchovy paste
2 cups sliced raw mushrooms	caramel color
⅓ cup sherry	¾ cup Colbert Sauce, page 120
2 cups Tomato Sauce, page 125	6 toasts, trimmed of crust

Poach the oysters in their own water. Remove the oysters and set aside reserving the liquor. Saute the green onions in the butter until they become limp, then add the mushrooms and sherry. Bring to a boil and add the Tomato Sauce and the oyster liquor.

In a separate pan caramelize the sugar with the water and add the vinegar and anchovy paste. Add this to the other ingredients and simmer for 30 minutes. Add the oysters and cook for a minute more.

To serve, spoon a portion containing six oysters on a slice of trimmed toast and top with two tablespoons of Colbert Sauce.

Serves 6.

HUITRES A LA FOCH
Oysters Foch

In December of 1921, Antoine's, in conjunction with the Knights of Columbus of New Orleans and Louisiana, played host to the great French World War I general named Foch. The repast was, in fact, a breakfast for which Jules created this dish to honor his important guest.

OYSTERS FOCH

6 slices toast, trimmed of crust	2 teaspoons salt
6 tablespoons canned pate de fois gras	½ teaspoon ground white pepper
3 dozen raw oysters	2 cups Colbert Sauce, page 120
1 cup finely ground yellow cornmeal	

Spread each toast with 1 tablespoon of pate de fois gras. Mix the cornmeal with the salt and pepper and roll the oysters in the mixture. Fry them in deep fat until they are cooked, and drain on absorbent paper. Place six on each toast and cover the oysters with Colbert Sauce.

Serves 6.

HUITRES BONNE FEMME
Oysters Bonne Femme

This dish differs from a classic Bonne Femme *both in the preparation of the sauce and in the use of the oysters.*

OYSTERS BONNE FEMME

3 dozen oysters in their water	salt and ground white pepper
3 tablespoons butter	1 cup lump crabmeat
3 tablespoons flour	3 tablespoons grated Swiss cheese
½ cup dry white wine	3 tablespoons grated Romano cheese
¾ cup chopped green onions	3 tablespoons grated Mozzarella cheese
1 tablespoon chopped parsley	¼ cup breadcrumbs

Poach the oysters in their own water. Strain and set aside, retaining the liquor.

Melt the butter in a saucepan and blend in the flour. Cook for two minutes or until the mixture becomes foamy. Add the white wine and green onions. Bring to a boil and add the oyster liquor.

Add the chopped parsley, season to taste with salt and pepper and simmer gently for 15 minutes. Carefully mix in the oysters and crabmeat. Adjust the seasoning, if necessary, and keep warm.

To serve, spoon the mixture into individual ovenproof dishes or ramekins. Mix the grated cheeses and breadcrumbs together and sprinkle over the top. Place in a preheated 400 °F oven until the cheese is melted and the top begins to brown.

Serves 6.

HUITRES BOURGUIGNONNE
Oysters Bourguignonne

A classic of French Cuisine adapted from snails to oysters.

OYSTERS BOURGUIGNONNE

3 dozen oysters in their own water
2 cups Bourguignonne Sauce, page 118

Poach the oysters in their own water. Remove the oysters from the liquor. Put six of the poached oysters in each of six small ovenproof dishes or ramekins. Cover the oysters with Bourguignonne Sauce and place in a heated 400°F oven until the sauce begins to bubble.

Serves 6.

HUITRES EN COQUILLE A LA ROCKEFELLER
Oysters Rockefeller

Oysters Rockefeller was created in 1899 by my great-grandfather Jules Alciatore. At that time there was a shortage of snails coming in from Europe to the United States and Jules was looking for a replacement. He wanted this replacement to be local in order to avoid any difficulty in procuring the product. He chose oysters. Jules was a pioneer in the art of cooked oysters, as they were rarely cooked before this time. He created a sauce with available green vegetable products, producing such a richness that he name it after one of the wealthiest men in the United States, John D. Rockefeller.

I have estimated that we have served over three million, five hundred thousand orders — quite a large number, considering that they have all been served in a single gourmet restaurant.

The original recipe is still a secret that I will not divulge. As many times as I have seen recipes printed in books and articles, I can honestly say that I have never found the original outside of Antoine's. If you care to concoct your version, I would tell you only that the sauce is basically a puree of a number of green vegetables other than spinach.

Bonne Chance!

CANAPE BALTHAZAR
Toast Balthazar

The French painter Casimir Alexandre Victor de Balthazar was born in the Moiselle in 1811 and died in Paris in 1875. He was a student of Paul de la Roche and exhibited his first works in 1833. From that year and until 1865 he was included in every major exposition in France. He was given his first major award in the year of 1840, which happens to be the same year that Antoine founded the restaurant. Antoine had admired the works of this artist in France before he came to the United States and wanted to create a dish which would be a culinary work of art as marvelous as were Balthazar's paintings. But there was more to this name than the painter. There was another Balthazar far earlier who was a biblical figure. This Balthazar was the son of Nabuchodonosor and was the last king of Babylonia. This particular Balthazar was far more colorful than our other. It seems that other than for his fall, he is best known for the wild, sumptuous orgies that he held in honor of himself in Babylonia. Both figures were taken into account by Antoine when he named this dish.

TOAST BALTHAZAR

2 tablespoons butter	2 tablespoons grated Mozzarella cheese
1 cup chopped green onions	1½ cups breadcrumbs
¾ cup white wine	salt and ground white pepper
2 cups raw oysters	4 tablespoons butter
¾ cup oyster water	4 tablespoons flour
2 tablespoons grated Swiss cheese	6 toasts, trimmed of crust
2 tablespoons grated Romano cheese	12 strips pimento

Saute the green onions in 2 tablespoons butter until they become limp. In another pot poach the oysters in the oyster water. Remove the oysters, retain the liquor, and chop them up.

Add the chopped oysters, wine and oyster liquor to the green onions and bring to a boil. Add the grated cheeses, ½ cup of the breadcrumbs and salt and pepper to taste.

In a small skillet, make a white roux with 4 tablespoons each of butter and flour. Blend the roux into the other ingredients and cook until mixture is thick enough to hold its own shape. Remove from heat and cool.

To serve, divide the mixture into 6 equal parts and shape into balls. Roll the balls in breadcrumbs and place each on a slice of toast. Cross 2 strips pimento over the top of each. Bake in a 375 °F oven for 15 minutes and serve.

Serves 6.

LES ESCARGOTS A LA BOURGUIGNONNE
Snails Bourguignonne

The French remember to flatter their ladies on occasion and in this case, probably in order to keep their stomachs full. A woman from the Burgundy country would be une Bourguignonne *and a woman from the Bordeaux country would be* une Bordelaise. *Just how flattered these ladies were to have a snail named after them is questionable. But I am sure the snails involved must certainly have been extremely delighted to have been prepared in such a delicious manner.*

SNAILS BOURGUIGNONNE

3 dozen canned snails
6 snail dishes
3½ cups Bourguignonne Sauce, page 118

Put a snail in each indentation of the snail dish. Cover each snail with Bourguignonne Sauce. Place in a hot 400 °F oven and bake 10 minutes until the sauce begins to bubble.

Serves 6.

LES ESCARGOTS A LA BORDELAISE
Snails Bordelaise

3 dozen canned snails
6 snail dishes
3½ cups Bordelaise Sauce
⅓ cup grated Mozzarella cheese

⅓ cup grated Swiss cheese
⅓ cup grated Romano cheese
½ cup breadcrumbs

Put a snail in each of the 6 indentations of each snail dish. Cover each snail with Bordelaise Sauce. Combine the grated cheeses and breadcrumbs and bake in a 400 °F oven for 10 minutes or until the cheese melts and the sauce begins to bubble.

Serves 6.

BORDELAISE SAUCE

2 tablespoons butter
¾ cup minced green onions
½ cup minced garlic

⅓ cup minced parsley
3 cups Marchand de Vin Sauce, page 126

Heat the butter and saute the green onions until they become limp. Add the garlic, parsley and Marchand de Vin Sauce and simmer for 20 minutes.

Makes 3½ cups.

CREVETTES A LA RICHMAN
Shrimp Richman

2 tablespoons butter
½ cup finely chopped carrots
⅓ cup finely chopped white onions
¼ cup finely chopped green onions
2 inch piece celery, finely chopped
2 cloves garlic, minced
⅓ cup tomato pulp
2½ cups raw peeled shrimp

¾ cup hot Fish Veloute, page 123
salt, ground white pepper and cayenne
   pepper
1 tablespoon chopped parsley
3 tablespoons grated Swiss Cheese
3 tablespoons grated Romano cheese
3 tablespoons grated Mozzarella cheese
¼ cup breadcrumbs

Melt the butter in a saucepan then add the carrots, white onion, green onions, celery, garlic and tomato pulp. Cook on a low fire for 5 minutes, then add the shrimp. Continue cooking until the vegetables are limp and the shrimp are cooked. Add the Fish Veloute and season to taste with salt, pepper and cayenne. Add the parsley and cook without boiling for 10 minutes more.

To serve, spoon the mixture into individual ovenproof dishes. Mix the grated cheese and breadcrumbs and sprinkle over the top. Bake in a preheated 400 °F oven until the cheese melts and the top begins to brown.

Serves 6.

CREVETTES A LA MARINIERE
Shrimp Mariniere

The most classic Mariniere would be made with moules *or* mussels. *Our preparation has changed not only to conform to local products but also to conform to local palates.*

SHRIMP MARINIERE

1 tablespoon butter
½ cup chopped green onions
⅓ cup white wine
2½ cups peeled raw shrimp

3 egg yolks
1½ cups warm Bechamel Sauce, page 123
salt, ground white pepper, and cayenne

Saute the green onions in the butter until they become limp, then add the wine. Bring to a boil, add the shrimp and cook together until shrimp are firm.

Mix the egg yolks with the warm Bechamel Sauce and the Bechamel with the shrimp. Add salt, pepper and cayenne to taste. Cook for a few minutes more without boiling.

Serves 6.

CREVETTES CARDINAL
Shrimp Cardinal

The reddish color, derived from the use of tomato paste in the preparation of the sauce for this dish, is reminiscent of one of nature's most striking creatures, the cardinal.

SHRIMP CARDINAL

6 tablespoons tomato paste
3 cups hot Shrimp Mariniere, page opposite
salt and cayenne pepper

Blend the tomato paste with the Shrimp Mariniere. Season with salt and cayenne pepper to taste.

Serves 6.

CREVETTES REMOULADE
Shrimp Remoulade

Quite different from the classic French Remoulade, our preparation has taken on the character of a purely Creole concoction.

SHRIMP REMOULADE

3 cups boiled shrimp, peeled
1 cup Remoulade Sauce, below
3 cups shredded lettuce

Blend the shrimp with the Remoulade Sauce, being careful not to break them. Chill in the refrigerator.

To serve, put ½ cup shredded lettuce on each of 6 cold appetizer plates. Spoon the shrimp onto the lettuce and serve.

Serves 6.

REMOULADE SAUCE

⅔ cup ketchup
½ teaspoon powdered mustard
2 tablespoons horseradish
1 tablespoon worcestershire

½ teaspoon Tabasco sauce
1 tablespoon minced green onions
1 tablespoon minced celery
1 tablespoon minced parsley

Combine all ingredients.

Makes 1 cup.

BOILED SHRIMP

2 tablespoons salt
1 teaspoon cayenne pepper
2 bay leaves

1½ quarts water
4½ cups raw headless shrimp, shells on

Add the salt, cayenne and bay leaves to the water and bring to a boil. Add the shrimp and when the water returns to a boil continue boiling for 5 minutes. Turn off the heat and soak for 10 minutes. Drain the shrimp and chill.

COCKTAIL AUX CREVETTES
Shrimp Cocktail

The word cocktail, which we use so frequently today, is actually a mispronunciation, and a misspelling of the word Coquetier, *which is French for egg cup. It seems the first cocktails served in the world were served in New Orleans in a small cafe, where the proprietor would mix some brandy with bitters and serve it in an egg cup. Through the years this word* Coquetier *gradually became a cocktail.*

Normally, in cuisine, when a dish is called a cocktail, it means that it is served in a cocktail glass. We have long ago eliminated the glass and now serve these dishes on small plates.

SHRIMP COCKTAIL

3 cups shredded lettuce
3 cups cold boiled shrimp, peeled
1½ cups Cocktail Sauce, page 117

Put ½ cup shredded lettuce on each plate and top with ½ cup shrimp. Serve with ¼ cup Cocktail Sauce in a small glass container on each plate.

Serves 6.

AVOCAT CREVETTES GARIBALDI
Avocado with Shrimp Garibaldi

Guiseppi Garibaldi was an Italian general born in Nice in 1807 and died in Caprera in 1882. He was an Italian patriot whose accomplishments were well known by both French and Italians. Antoine exhibited his admiration for the man with the creation of this dish.

AVOCADO WITH SHRIMP GARIBALDI

3 cups shredded lettuce
3 avocados, peeled and halved

3 cups Shrimp Ravigote
1½ cups Vinaigrette Sauce, page 117

Place each avocado half on a bed of shredded lettuce. Fill with ½ cup Shrimp Ravigote and pour over ¼ cup Vinaigrette Sauce.

Serves 6.

SHRIMP RAVIGOTE

Prepare the same way as Crabmeat Ravigote, substituting the crabmeat with peeled boiled shrimp. See page opposite.

TOMATE FRAPPEE A LA JULES CESAR
Chilled Tomato Jules Cesar

When Jules Alciatore had his first son, he took the child, christened him with champagne and called him Jules Cesar, for it would be this child, as he thought, that would bear the responsibility for the continuation of Antoine's. As fate had it, Jules Cesar Alciatore did not take on the operation of Antoine's, but rather, became a professor of romance languages, his true heart's desire. The dish still remains as tribute from father Jules Louis to son Jules Cesar.

CHILLED TOMATO JULES CESAR

6 large tomatoes
3 cups Crabmeat Ravigote

3 cups shredded lettuce
1½ cups Vinaigrette Sauce, page 117

Cut off the tops of the tomatoes and remove the seeds and most of the pulp with a spoon. As you do this, be sure to scoop out one nicely rounded ball of pulp (as for melon balls) from each tomato to use as garnish. Fill each tomato with ½ cup Crab Ravigote and top with a ball of pulp. Chill the tomato or *frappee*, meaning to ice.

To serve, place each tomato on a bed of chopped lettuce and pour over some Vinaigrette Sauce.

Serves 6.

CHAIR DE CRABES RAVIGOTE
Crabmeat Ravigote

Ravigote comes from the French word ravigoter, *which means to invigorate someone. This sauce called Ravigote is composed of ingredients which would, of course, invigorate or revitalize the palate.*

CRABMEAT RAVIGOTE

4½ cups lump crabmeat
1 cup Ravigote Sauce

Blend the crabmeat with the Ravigote Sauce, being very careful not to break up the crabmeat. Chill in the refrigerator and serve on a bed of shredded lettuce.

Serves 6.

RAVIGOTE SAUCE

1 cup Mayonnaise, page 117
1½ tablespoons minced bell pepper
1½ tablespoons minced green onions
1½ tablespoons minced anchovies
1½ tablespoons minced pimento

Mix all ingredients together and chill.

Makes almost 1¼ cups.

AVOCAT A LA CHAIR DE CRABES GARIBALDI
Avocado with Crabmeat Garibaldi

3 cups shredded lettuce

3 avocados, peeled and halved

3 cups Crabmeat Ravigote, page 41

1½ cups Vinaigrette Sauce, page 117

Place each avocado half on a bed of shredded lettuce. Fill with ½ cup Crabmeat Ravigote and pour over ¼ cup Vinaigrette Sauce.

Serves 6.

COCKTAIL A LA CHAIR DE CRABES
Crabmeat Cocktail

Again the cocktail appears, this time with crabmeat.

CRABMEAT COCKTAIL

3 cups shredded lettuce

3 cups cold crabmeat

1½ cups Cocktail Sauce, page 117

Put ½ cup shredded lettuce on each plate and top with ½ cup crabmeat. Serve with ¼ cup Cocktail Sauce in a small glass container on each plate.

Serves 6.

CHAIR DE CRABES ST. PIERRE
Crabmeat St. Peter

I feel certain that dear Jules is enjoying his everlasting life in heaven. After all, St. Peter would certainly not resist the entry of the man who had honored him so well with this dish.

CRABMEAT ST. PETER

3 cups crabmeat
1½ cups warm Creole Sauce, page 124
salt and cayenne pepper
3 tablespoons grated Swiss cheese

3 tablespoons grated Romano cheese
3 tablespoons grated Mozzarella cheese
¼ cup breadcrumbs

Combine the crabmeat with the warm Creole Sauce. Add salt and cayenne pepper if needed and heat for a minute.

Spoon the mixture into individual ovenproof dishes. Combine the grated cheeses and breadcrumbs and sprinkle over the top.

Bake in a preheated 400 °F oven until the top begins to brown.

Serves 6.

CHAIR DE CRABES AU GRATIN
Crabmeat au Gratin

When a dish is prepared au gratin *it usually means that the dish will be made with a crust across the top of grated cheese and breadcrumbs and placed in an intense heat to cook. Our preparation differs very little from the general rule.*

CRABMEAT AU GRATIN

1 cup hot Bechamel Sauce, page 123
2 cups lump crabmeat
salt and ground white pepper
3 tablespoons grated Swiss cheese

3 tablespoons grated Romano cheese
3 tablespoons grated Mozzarella cheese
¼ cup breadcrumbs

Blend the Bechamel Sauce and the crabmeat. Add salt and pepper to taste and heat for a minute. Spoon the mixture into 6 small ovenproof dishes.

Combine the grated cheeses and breadcrumbs and sprinkle over the top. Bake in a preheated 400 °F oven until top begins to brown.

Serves 6.

CANAPE ST. ANTOINE
Toast St. Antoine

One of the institutors of the monastic life was St. Antoine, born in the year 251 of a wealthy family in the village of Coma, Egypt. At the age of twenty he distributed his wealth to the poor and retired to the deserts of the Thebaid, where he was followed by a number of Christians. He founded several monasteries and governed them for a long time.

Nearing the end of his career, he took refuge in the solitude of the deepest area of the desert with two preferred disciples. He died in 356 at the age of 105 years.

During the last fifteen years of his life in the desert he was obsessed by fantastic visions which have become quite celebrated in the ecclesiastical tradition and have often inspired the artists. Fortunately for St. Antoine, this canape was not one of his visions for he would certainly have fallen had he been tempted by this offering.

TOAST ST. ANTOINE

2 tablespoons butter
1 cup chopped green onions
½ cup white wine
2 cups crabmeat
½ cup Bechamel Sauce, page 123
2 tablespoons grated Swiss cheese
2 tablespoons grated Romano cheese
2 tablespoons grated Mozzarella cheese
1½ cups breadcrumbs
salt and ground white pepper to taste
6 toasts, trimmed of crusts
12 anchovy fillets

Saute the green onions in the butter until they become limp. Add the white wine and crabmeat and bring to a boil. Blend in the Bechamel Sauce, the grated cheeses, and ½ cup of the breadcrumbs. Season to taste with salt and pepper.

Continue cooking until the mixture can hold its own shape. Cool slightly.

Divide into six equal parts and shape into balls. Roll the balls in breadcrumbs and place them on the toasts. Cross 2 anchovy fillets over the top of each and bake in a 375 °F oven for 15 minutes.

Serves 6.

ECREVISSES A LA MARINIERE
Crayfish Mariniere

Again we see our Mariniere Sauce, this time in preparation with a great delicacy of the world, so bountiful in this area, the crayfish.

CRAYFISH MARINIERE

Prepare the same way as Shrimp Mariniere, substituting crayfish tails for the shrimp. Page 36.

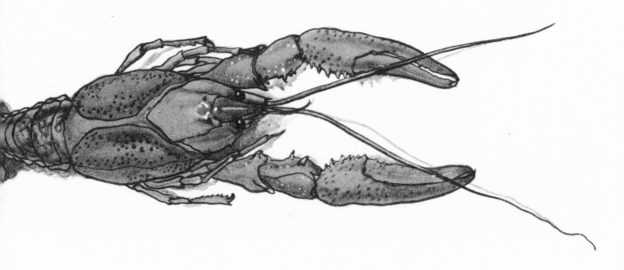

ECREVISSES A LA CARDINAL
Crayfish Cardinal

Prepare the same way as the Shrimp Cardinal, substituting crayfish tails for the shrimp. Page 37.

CHAMPIGNONS SUR TOSTE
Mushrooms on Toast

There is nothing which compares in lightness or delicacy to the champignon *or* mushroom.

MUSHROOMS ON TOAST

1 stick butter

salt and ground white pepper

3 cups whole mushroom tops, washed

6 toasts, trimmed of crust

Heat the butter until hot. Saute the mushrooms quickly with just a sprinkling of salt and pepper and spoon onto the toasts. Pour the butter from the pan over the mushrooms.

Serves 6.

CHAMPIGNONS SOUS CLOCHE
Mushrooms under Glass

Beneath a glass bell appears the champignon *prepared in a light sauce with sherry.*

MUSHROOMS UNDER GLASS

1 stick butter
6 cups sliced mushrooms
½ cup sherry

2 cups Bechamel Sauce, page 123
salt and ground white pepper
6 toasts, trimmed of crust

Melt the butter and saute the mushrooms until they become limp. Add the sherry and bring to a boil. Add the Bechamel Sauce, and season to taste with salt and pepper. Simmer gently for 15 minutes.

Serve on toast under a glass bell.

Serves 6.

ANCHOIS SUR CANAPE
Anchovy Canape

Nothing could be more appealing to the lover of the anchovy, and no dish could be more simple.

ANCHOVY CANAPE

6 slices toast
3 dozen anchovy fillets

6 lettuce leaves
3 hard-boiled eggs, finely chopped

Cover each toast with 6 anchovy fillets. Trim the crusts from the toasts with a sharp knife. Cut the toasts in fours. Garnish each plate with a lettuce leaf filled with some of the chopped hard-boiled egg.

Serves 6.

CANAPE ROTHSCHILD
Toast Rothschild

Of German origin, the Rothschilds were a powerful and wealthy family of bankers in the nineteenth century. Antoine created the Canape Rothschild for them.

TOAST ROTHSCHILD

6 tablespoons pate de foie gras
6 slices toast
1 hard-boiled egg, chopped

3 tablespoons capers
6 (½'') cubes truffles

Spread each toast with 1 tablespoon pate de foie gras. Sprinkle some chopped hard boiled egg around the edges of the toasts. Top each with ½ tablespoon capers and place a cube of truffle in the center. Put the toasts on a baking pan and place in a hot 400°F. oven for two minutes.

Serves 6.

CAVIAR SUR CANAPE
Caviar on Toast

Caviar is made by salting or marinating the roe or eggs of the fish called the sturgeon. As caviar is a great delicacy in the world, it is best served in the simple fashion outlined here.

CAVIAR ON TOAST

6 slices toast	1 cup chopped onion
6 tablespoons caviar	3 lemons, halved
3 hard-boiled eggs, finely chopped	6 lettuce leaves

Spread 1 tablespoon caviar on each toast and cut off the crusts. Cut the toasts in fours and place on chilled serving dishes.

Garnish each plate with ½ lemon and a lettuce leaf filled with chopped egg and onions.

Serves 6.

FOIE GRAS DE STRASBOURG A LA GELEE
Goose Liver from Strasbourg with Jellied Consomme

Strasbourg, located in the northeast of France, has long been famous for its production of foie gras, *which literally means* fat liver. *These fat livers, generally of goose, are developed through extraordinary methods of feeding the geese before they are taken to market. The result is perhaps equaled only by caviar as one of the world's great delicacies.*

GOOSE LIVER FROM STRASBOURG WITH JELLIED CONSOMME

6 (½'') slices foie gras, canned
3 cups Jellied Consomme
6 parsley sprigs

Chill the foie gras, the Jellied Consomme, and the plates on which you are going to serve the foie gras.

Put the foie gras on the plates and surround with Jellied Consomme, cut into ½ inch cubes. Garnish with parsley.

Serves 6.

JELLIED CONSOMME

Soften two packets gelatin in ⅓ cup white wine and stir into 3 cups hot consomme. Chill. See Consomme, page 58.

POTAGES
Soups

Harold Marchand is using a fifty-
year-old copper pot to make
turtle soup, a favorite specialty
in New Orleans.

Bisques and *Gumbos* *are an important part of our local cuisine, and a part of which we are particularly proud.*

Jules Alciatore was particularly proud of his soups. So proud, in fact, that when Sarah Bernhardt was performing at the French Opera House (destroyed by fire in 1919) he would bring her a small tureen of soup each night before her performance.

At the close of her engagement in New Orleans the renowned actress kissed Jules enthusiastically and said, ''If my New Orleans engagement has been a success, my dear Jules, it is because you have provided me with the strength to make it so.''

Years later during the twenties, the elderly Sarah Bernhardt was making her last tour of the United States and again played New Orleans, at the Orpheum Theatre. In memory of her first visit many years before, Jules, himself in his seventies, brought her a bowl of soup which is said to have touched her more than the standing ovation of the audience that evening.

GOMBO CREOLE
Creole Gumbo

The Bouillabaisse of Louisiana appears in many forms. Ours is the classic creole seafood gumbo.

CREOLE GUMBO

¾ stick butter
2 cups chopped green onions
3 crabs (top shell discarded,
    cut in 4 pieces)
2 cups sliced okra
1 cup chopped white onions
2 cups raw peeled shrimp
2 cups raw oysters

1 cup chopped tomato pulp
2 cups tomato juice
1½ quarts Fish Stock, page 115
3 tablespoons butter
3 tablespoons flour
1 tablespoon File (sassafras)
salt, pepper and cayenne
3 cups cooked rice

Melt the butter and saute the green onions, okra, white onions and crabs. In a separate pot put the shrimp, oysters, tomatoes and tomato juice with 1½ quarts of Fish Stock and bring to a boil. Let boil for a minute, then add to the first pot. In a small skillet cook the butter and flour together until brown. Blend this brown roux with the File and some of the gumbo liquid and add to the gumbo. Add salt and pepper and cayenne to taste. Simmer for 1½ hours.

To serve, pour 1½ cups of gumbo into each bowl over ½ cup rice.

Serves 6.

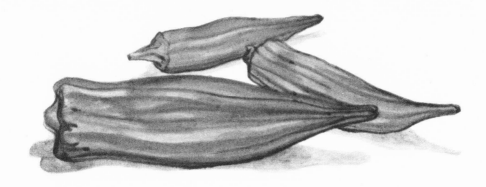

POTAGE TORTUE AU SHERRY
Turtle Soup with Sherry

1 stick butter
1 pound turtle meat cut into
   ½ inch cubes
2 cups finely chopped onions
⅓ cup finely chopped celery
2 cups tomato pulp
1 lemon

1 cup sherry
3 cups Espagnole Sauce, page 126
1 quart Beef Stock, page 116
2 bay leaves
2 tablespoons chopped parsley
salt and ground white pepper

Melt the butter in a large soup pot and saute the turtle meat until it is golden brown. Add the onions and cook until they begin to color. Add the celery and cook until it becomes soft. Add the tomato pulp and cook for five minutes more.

Squeeze the juice from the lemon and add it to the pot. Discard the seeds. Mince finely the pulp and peel of the lemon. Add this and all remaining ingredients to the soup pot and simmer gently for 1½-2 hours.

Serves 6.

BISQUE DES ECREVISSES CARDINAL
Crayfish Bisque Cardinal

⅓ cup flour
⅓ cup butter
2 pounds whole live crayfish
1 stick butter
1 cup chopped carrots
1 cup chopped white onions

½ cup chopped green onions
¾ cup tomato pulp
2 quarts Fish Stock, page 115
salt, ground white pepper and cayenne
12 stuffed crayfish heads

Make a brown roux with ⅓ cup flour and ⅓ cup butter. Set aside. Drop the live crayfish into a pot of boiling salted water and cook for two minutes. Remove the crayfish from the water and carefully remove at least 12 heads. Set these aside for stuffing.

Put the remainder of the crayfish in a large heavy soup pot. Pound the crayfish in the bottom of the pot until they are crushed into a pulp. Add the butter and put the pot on the fire. When the butter is melted and hot, add the carrots, white onions and green onions. Cook together until the vegetables begin to color. Then add the tomatoes.

Cook for about five minutes more and stir in the roux. Add the Fish Stock, blending as you add. Bring to a boil. Reduce to a simmer and add salt, pepper and cayenne to taste. Cook for one hour, strain and serve with 2 stuffed crayfish heads in each bowl.

Serves 6.

STUFFED CRAYFISH HEADS

1 tablespoon butter
½ cup chopped green onions
⅓ cup white wine
¾ cup chopped crayfish tails,
    meat only
⅓ cup Bechamel Sauce, page 123
1 tablespoon grated Swiss cheese

1 tablespoon grated Romano cheese
1 tablespoon grated Mozzarella cheese
¼ cup breadcrumbs
salt and ground white pepper
12 cleaned crayfish heads
bread crumbs

Saute the green onions in the butter until they become limp. Add the white wine and chopped crayfish tails and bring to a boil. Add the Bechamel Sauce, the Swiss, Romano and Mozzarella cheeses and the breadcrumbs. Season with salt and pepper to taste. Cook until the mixture can hold its own shape.

Remove from the heat and stuff the cleaned crayfish heads with the mixture. Cover exposed areas of stuffing with breadcrumbs. Hold in the oven to keep warm.

Makes 12 heads.

BISQUE DES CREVETTES
Shrimp Bisque

This bisque is prepared in the same way as Crayfish Bisque, substituting the same quantity of shrimp for crayfish. For Shrimp Bisque we do not use the stuffed heads.

CONSOMME CHAUD AU VERMICELLE
Hot Consomme with Vermicelli

1 pound ground lean beef	¼ teaspoon dried thyme
2 tablespoons butter	4 cloves
1 cup chopped onion	3 packets gelatin
1 cup chopped carrots	salt and ground white pepper
½ cup chopped celery	3 egg whites
3 quarts Beef Stock, page 116	½ cup water
2 bay leaves	¼ pound vermicelli (thin spaghetti)

Brown the meat in the bottom of a large soup pot with a little butter. Add the onions, carrots, celery, beef stock, bay leaves, thyme, cloves and gelatin. Bring to a boil then turn down the fire to a very slight simmer. Cook for 1 hour, skimming the fat off the top, then season to taste with salt and pepper.

Combine 3 egg whites with ½ cup water and stir into the consomme. Continue simmering for about 10 minutes. Turn off the heat, let the consomme cool slightly and pour it through several thicknesses of cheesecloth.

To serve, put the consomme into a large pot and bring to a boil. Break ¼ pound vermicelli into the consomme and continue boiling until the vermicelli is tender. Adjust seasoning and serve.

Serves 6.

CONSOMME FROID EN TASSE
Cold Consomme in a Cup

1½ quarts Consomme
3 lemons, halved

Chill the consomme until it gels. Spoon it into cups and serve with a lemon half on each plate.

Serves 6.

VICHYSSOISE
Cold Potato Soup

4 potatoes
1 ham bone or slice of ham
5 cups Chicken Stock, page 115

salt and ground white pepper
2 cups half and half
3 tablespoons chopped chives

Peel the potatoes, cut them into pieces and put them in a pot with the ham bone and the chicken stock. Bring to a slight simmer and add a tablespoon of salt and ½ teaspoon of pepper. Cook for about 30 minutes or until potatoes are soft.

Put the half and half in another pot and heat almost to a boil. Set aside. Pass the potatoes, stock and half and half through a strainer, adjust the seasoning and chill. Serve garnished with chopped chives.

Serves 6.

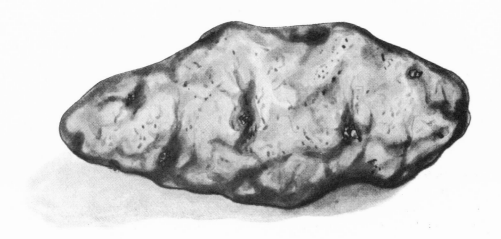

SOUPE A L'OIGNON GRATINE
Onion Soup with Cheese

¾ stick butter
4 cups onion, roughly chopped
2 tablespoons flour
2 quarts rich Beef Stock, page 116
salt and ground white pepper

6 toasts, trimmed of crust
⅓ cup grated Swiss cheese
⅓ cup grated Romano cheese
⅓ cup grated American cheese
⅓ cup grated Cheddar cheese

Melt the butter in the bottom of a large soup pot and cook the onions until they are golden brown in color. Stir in the flour and cook for about two minutes.

Add the beef stock and bring to a boil. Turn down the fire and simmer gently for 30 minutes. Salt and pepper to taste.

To serve, ladle some soup into each bowl. Float the toast on top and cover with the ground cheese mixture. Put the bowls under a broiler until the cheese is melted and begins to brown.

Serves 6.

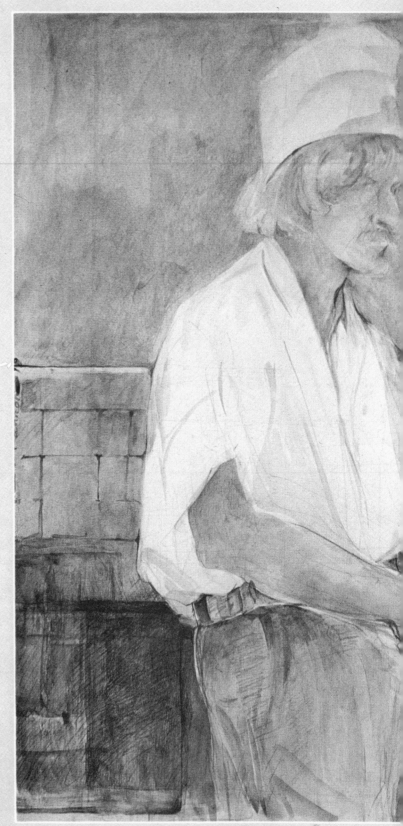

Night chef John DuBroc is filleting trout in a special room in the back of Antoine's kitchen, used just for the preparation of fish, and known affectionately as "the fish hole."

POISSONS
Fish and Seafood

We are extremely fortunate to have an abundant variety of available local seafood. For that reason our cuisine is basically a seafood cuisine, developed through a compatible marriage of French, Spanish and African influences.

FILET DE TRUITE MEUNIERE
Trout Meuniere

1½ cups half and half
3 whole eggs
1 teaspoon salt
½ teaspoon ground white pepper

6 skinned trout fillets, 8 ounces each
flour
1¼ cups butter
¾ cup lemon juice

Make a batter by combining the half and half, eggs, salt and pepper. Dredge the trout fillets in flour, dip them in the batter, then dredge them in flour again. Fry in deep fat until they are golden brown and rise to the surface of the fat.

Heat the butter until it begins to color.

Serve the trout fillets with the butter and lemon juice poured over.

Serves 6.

FILET DE TRUITE AMANDINE
Trout Amandine

3 cups sliced almonds
1½ cups butter
1½ cups half and half
3 whole eggs

1 teaspoon salt
½ teaspoon ground white pepper
6 skinned trout fillets, 8 ounces each
flour

Saute the almonds in the butter until they become golden brown. Keep warm. Make a batter by combining the half and half, eggs, salt and pepper. Dredge the trout fillets in flour, then dip into the batter, then into the flour again. Fry in deep fat until golden brown and float in the fat.

Drain on absorbent paper and serve topped with the almonds and butter.

Serves 6.

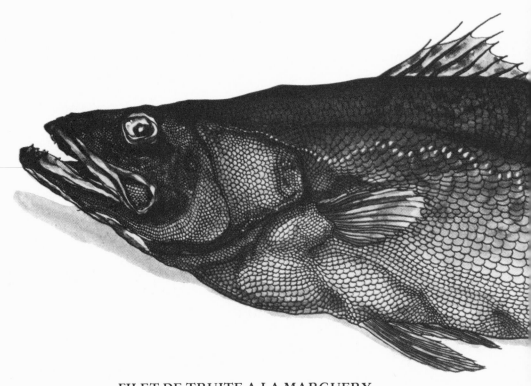

FILET DE TRUITE A LA MARGUERY
Trout Marguery

3 tablespoons butter
½ cup chopped green onions
1 cup sliced mushrooms
1 cup raw peeled shrimp
1½ cups white wine
2 cups Bechamel Sauce, page 123
salt and ground white pepper
6 skinned trout fillets, 6 ounces each

1 onion, sliced
5 whole black peppercorns
2 bay leaves
juice of 1 lemon
water
4 egg yolks
6 sprigs parsley

Saute the green onions and mushrooms in the butter until they become limp. Add the shrimp and 1 cup of the white wine and bring to a boil; blend in the Bechamel Sauce. Season to taste with salt and ground white pepper. Keep warm.

Poach the trout fillets in a shallow pan with the sliced onion, 2 teaspoons salt, the whole black peppercorns, the bay leaves, the lemon juice, the remaining ½ cup wine and enough water to cover. Bring to a boil then simmer until the fillets are tender. Remove from the poaching liquid and keep warm.

Mix the egg yolks into the Marguery Sauce and adjust seasoning. Cook for 2 minutes without boiling. Spoon the sauce over the poached trout fillets and serve, garnished with parsley sprigs.

Serves 6.

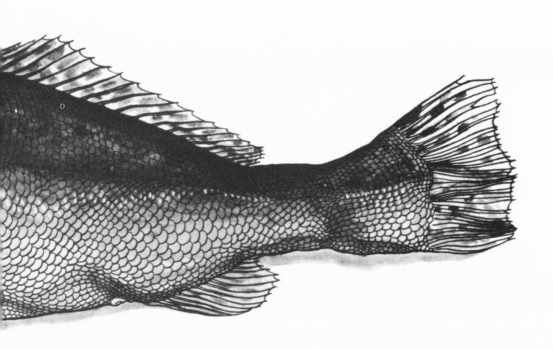

FILET DE TRUITE AU VIN BLANC
Trout in White Wine Sauce

1 cup raw oysters in their own water
2 tablespoons butter
½ cup chopped green onions
¾ cup raw peeled shrimp
1½ cups white wine
1½ cups Fish Veloute Sauce, page 123
salt and cayenne pepper
6 skinned trout fillets, 6 ounces each
1 onion, sliced

5 whole black peppercorns
2 bay leaves
juice from 1 lemon
water
3 tablespoons grated Swiss cheese
3 tablespoons grated Romano cheese
3 tablespoons grated Mozzarella cheese
¼ cup breadcrumbs

Poach the oysters in their own water, strain and set aside.

Saute the green onions in butter until they become limp. Add the shrimp and 1 cup of the white wine and bring to a boil. Blend in the fish Veloute Sauce and the cooked oysters and season to taste with salt and cayenne pepper. Keep warm.

Poach the trout fillets in a shallow pan with the sliced onion, 2 teaspoons salt, the whole black peppercorns, the remaining ½ cup wine, the bay leaves, the lemon juice and enough water to cover. Bring the water to a boil then reduce to a simmer until the fillets are tender. Remove from the poaching liquid, drain and place on serving dishes.

Spoon the sauce over the trout fillets. Mix the grated cheeses and breadcrumbs together and sprinkle this over the fish. Pass under a broiler flame to melt the cheese and serve.

Serves 6.

FILET DE TRUITE FLORENTINE
Trout Florentine

6 skinned trout fillets, 6 ounces each
1 onions, sliced
2 teaspoons salt
5 whole black peppercorns
2 bay leaves
juice of 1 lemon
½ cup white wine

3 cups Creamed Spinach, page 137
2 cups Hollandaise Sauce, page 119
3 tablespoons grated Swiss cheese
3 tablespoons grated Romano cheese
3 tablespoons grated Mozzarella cheese
¼ cup breadcrumbs

Poach the trout fillets in a shallow pan with the sliced onion, salt, the whole black peppercorns, the bay leaves, the lemon juice, the wine and enough water to cover. Remove from the liquid and keep warm.

Put ½ cup warm Creamed Spinach in the bottom of each individual ovenproof dish. Lay a trout fillet over each bed of creamed spinach and top with ⅓ cup Hollandaise Sauce.

Combine the grated cheeses and breadcrumbs and sprinkle over the top. Place under a broiler flame to melt the cheese.

Serves 6.

POMPANO GRILLE
Grilled Pompano

6 pompano fillets, 8 ounces each	1½ cups melted butter
oil	6 parsley sprigs
salt	3 lemons, halved

Brush the pompano fillets with oil and salt lightly. Cook on a grill or in a heavy iron skillet. Cook the pompano for about three minutes on each side, or until done. Garnish each plate with a parsley sprig and ½ lemon. Serve with melted butter poured over.

Serves 6.

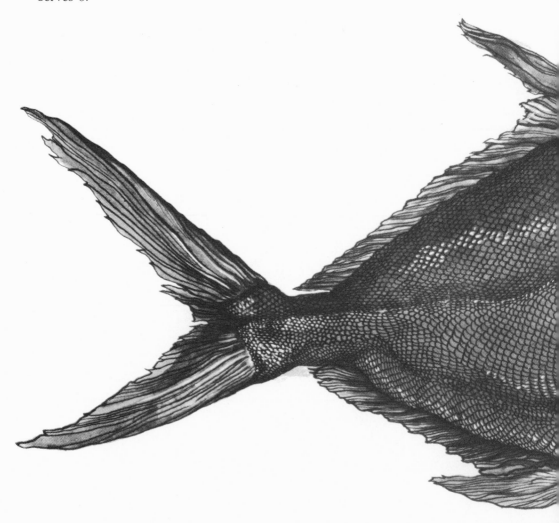

POMPANO PONTCHARTRAIN
Pompano with Crabmeat

Proceed the same as for Pompano Grille, but serve each fillet of pompano topped with ½ cup good lump crabmeat, which you have heated with 3 tablespoons butter. See Pompano Grille, opposite page.

POMPANO AMANDINE
Pompano with Almonds

Prepare the same way as Trout Amandine, substituting 8-ounce pompano fillets for the trout fillets. See page 65.

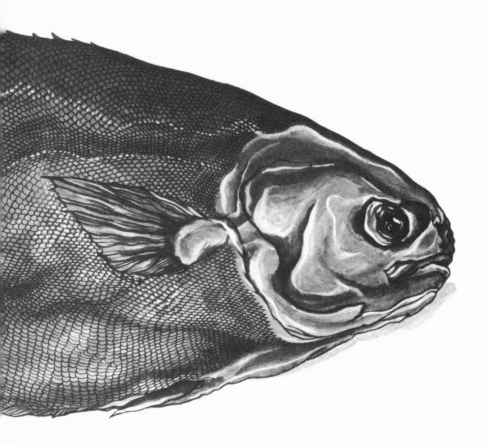

POMPANO A LA MARINIERE
Pompano Mariniere

3 tablespoons butter
1½ cups chopped green onions
1½ cups white wine
2½ cups Bechamel Sauce, page 123
salt, ground white pepper and cayenne
6 skinned pompano fillets, 6 ounces each

1 onion, sliced
5 whole black peppercorns
2 bay leaves
juice of 1 lemon
water
6 egg yolks
6 parsley sprigs

Saute the green onions in the butter until they become limp. Add 1 cup of the wine and bring to a boil; blend in the Bechamel Sauce. Season to taste with salt and white pepper and cayenne.

Poach the pompano fillets in a shallow pan with the sliced onion, 2 teaspoons salt, the whole black peppercorns, the remaining ½ cup white wine, the bay leaves, the lemon juice and enough water to cover. Remove from the cooking liquid and keep warm.

Blend the egg yolks into the sauce and cook for 2 minutes more without boiling. Adjust seasoning if necessary.

Serve the poached pompano fillets with the sauce poured over, and garnished with a sprig of parsley.

Serves 6.

POMPANO EN PAPILLOTE
Pompano in a Paper Bag

3 tablespoons butter	6 skinned pompano fillets, 6 ounces each
1 cup chopped green onions	1 onion, sliced
1 cup raw peeled shrimp	5 whole black peppercorns
1½ cups white wine	2 bay leaves
2 cups Fish Veloute Sauce, page 123	juice from 1 lemon
1 cup lump crabmeat	water
salt, ground white pepper and cayenne	white parchment paper

Melt the butter and saute the green onions until they become limp. Add the raw shrimp, 1 cup of the wine and bring to a boil. Blend in the Veloute Sauce and the crabmeat. Season to taste with salt, pepper and cayenne. Simmer gently for 10 minutes, then let cool.

Poach the pompano fillets in a shallow pan with the sliced onion, 2 teaspoons salt, the whole black peppercorns, the remaining ½ cup wine, the bay leaves, the lemon juice and enough water to cover. Remove the fillets from the poaching liquid and keep warm.

From the white parchment paper cut 6 heart-shaped pieces about 10 inches high and 14 inches wide.

Spoon some of the sauce onto the center of one half of the heart-shaped paper and top with a pompano fillet. Fold the other half of the paper over the top and seal the edges by folding together.

Place these on an oiled baking pan, and into a 400 °F oven for 15 minutes or until the paper begins to brown.

Bring to the table and cut the top of the paper open.
Serves 6.

73

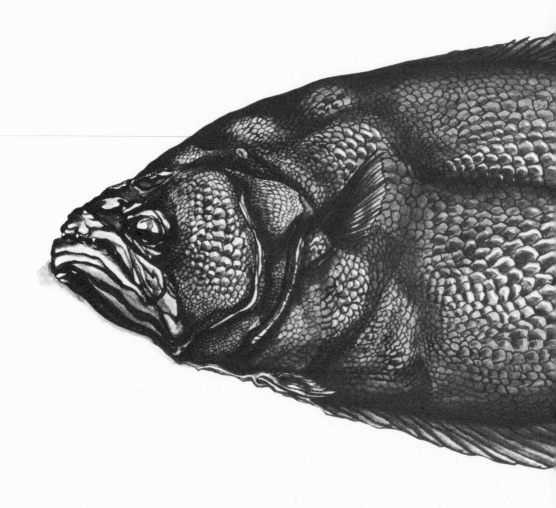

FILET DE FLET COLBERT
Fillet of Flounder with Colbert Sauce

1½ cups half and half
3 whole eggs
1 teaspoon salt
½ teaspoon ground white pepper

6 skinned flounder filets, 8 ounces each
flour
breadcrumbs
2 cups Colbert Sauce, page 120

Make a batter by combining the half and half, the eggs, salt and pepper. Dip the flounder fillets in flour, then batter, then breadcrumbs. Fry in deep fat until they are golden brown and float to the surface of the fat.

Drain on absorbent paper and serve with Colbert Sauce.

Serves 6.

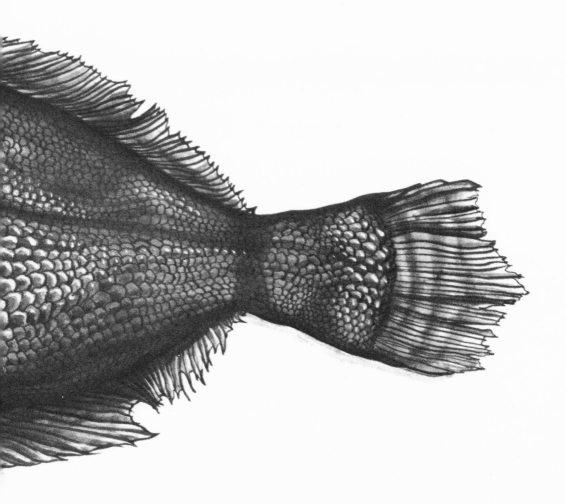

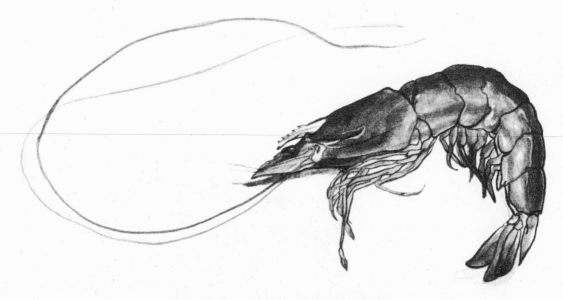

CREVETTES A LA CREOLE
Shrimp Creole

3 pounds raw shrimp, peeled
1 stick butter
salt and cayenne pepper

3 cups Creole Sauce, page 124
3 cups hot cooked rice

Heat the butter and saute the shrimp with a little salt and cayenne pepper until the shrimp become firm. Add the Creole Sauce and simmer together for 20 minutes.

Serve the shrimp and sauce with ½ cup hot cooked rice on each plate.

Serves 6.

SALADE DE CREVETTES
Shrimp Salad

8 cups cold boiled shrimp, peeled, page 38
1 cup chopped green onions
1 teaspoon salt
½ teaspoon ground white pepper
6 lettuce leaves

6 tablespoons Mayonnaise, page 117
6 bell pepper rings
6 slices tomato, halved
2 cups Vinaigrette Sauce, page 117

Mix the shrimp with the chopped green onions, salt and pepper and divide into 6 portions. Place each portion on a lettuce leaf and top with a tablespoon mayonnaise and a ring of bell pepper. Garnish with a slice of tomato cut in half. Chill and serve cold with Vinaigrette Sauce.

Serves 6.

LANGOUSTE GRILLEE
Grilled Rock Lobster

1 rock lobster, 2 pounds
oil
salt

⅓ cup melted butter
1 lemon, halved

Split the lobster in half and clean the head of one half. Remove the tail meat from the other half and stuff it into the head of the cleaned half. Discard the empty shell. Brush the exposed meat with oil and salt lightly. Cook on a grill or in a heavy iron skillet, first the meat side, then the shell side, until the lobster is done.

Serve with 2 lemon halves and ⅓ cup hot melted butter to dip the lobster meat into.

Serves 1.

LANGOUSTE SAUTEE
Sauteed Rock Lobster

2 cups butter
8 cups rock lobster meat, cut into 1 inch cubes
salt and ground white pepper

Put the butter in a large saute pan and heat until fairly hot. Add the lobster meat and saute for a few minutes.

Season lightly with salt and pepper and serve with the cooking butter.

Serves 6.

LANGOUSTE THERMIDOR
Rock Lobster Thermidor

5 cups lobster meat	3 tablespoons grated Swiss cheese
1½ cups sherry	3 tablespoons grated Romano cheese
3 cups warm Bechamel Sauce, page 123	3 tablespoons grated Mozzarella cheese
salt and ground white pepper	¼ cup breadcrumbs

Cut the lobster meat into 1-inch pieces. Put these pieces and the sherry into a pot and boil, stirring the lobster occasionally until the sherry is reduced by half. Add the Bechamel Sauce and season to taste with salt and pepper. Continue cooking on a low heat for a few minutes more.

Spoon the mixture into individual ovenproof dishes. Combine the cheeses and breadcrumbs and sprinkle over the top.

Place in a 400 °F oven until the cheese is melted and the top begins to brown.

Serves 6.

CRABES MOUS GRILLES
Grilled Soft-Shell Crabs

1 dozen cleaned and dressed soft-
   shell crabs
oil

salt
2 cups hot melted butter
6 lemons, halved

Brush the crabs with oil and salt lightly. Cook on a grill or in a heavy iron skillet. Cook on one side then turn the crabs over and finish cooking on the other side.

Serve 2 crabs per person with melted butter and lemon halves.

Serves 6.

CRABES MOUS FRITS
Fried Soft-Shell Crabs

1½ cups half and half
3 whole eggs
1 teaspoon salt
½ teaspoon ground white pepper

1 dozen dressed soft-shell crabs
flour
6 lemons, halved

Make a batter by combining the half and half, eggs, salt and pepper. Dredge the crabs in flour, dip them into the batter, and dredge in flour again. Fry in deep fat until golden brown and completely cooked.

Drain on absorbent paper and serve, garnished with 2 lemon halves.

Serves 6.

CRABES MOUS AMANDINE
Soft-Shell Crab with Almonds

3 cups sliced toasted almonds
1½ cups butter
1½ cups half and half
3 whole eggs

1 teaspoon salt
½ teaspoon ground white pepper
1 dozen dressed soft-shell crabs
flour

Saute the almonds in the butter until they become golden brown. Keep warm.

Make a batter by combining the half and half, eggs, salt and pepper. Dredge the crabs in flour, then into the batter, then back into the flour again. Fry in deep fat until golden brown and completely cooked.

Drain the crabs on absorbent paper and serve topped with the almonds and butter.

Serves 6.

SALADE DE CHAIR DE CRABES
Crabmeat Salad

8 cups lump crabmeat
1 cup chopped green onions
1 tablespoon salt
1 teaspoon ground white pepper
6 lettuce leaves

6 tablespoons Mayonnaise, page 117
6 bell pepper rings
6 slices tomato, halved
2 cups Vinaigrette Sauce, page 117

Mix the crabmeat with the chopped green onions, salt and pepper and divide into 6 portions. Place each portion on a lettuce leaf and top with a tablespoon mayonaise and a ring of bell pepper. Garnish with a slice of tomato cut in half. Chill and serve cold with Vinaigrette Sauce.

Serves 6.

CHAIR DE CRABES RAVIGOTE
Hot Crabmeat Ravigote

¼ cup minced bell pepper
¼ cup minced green onion
¼ cup minced pimento
¼ cup minced anchovies
2½ cups hot Bechamel Sauce, page 123
6 cups lump crabmeat

salt and ground white pepper
3 tablespoons grated Swiss cheese
3 tablespoons grated Romano cheese
3 tablespoons grated Mozzarella cheese
⅓ cup breadcrumbs

Combine the bell pepper, green onions, pimento, and anchovies in a saucepan with the Bechamel Sauce. Blend in the crabmeat and heat together until hot. Add salt and pepper if needed.

Spoon the mixture into individual ovenproof dishes. Combine the grated cheeses and breadcrumbs and sprinkle over the top.

Bake in a preheated 400 °F oven until the cheese is melted and the top begins to brown.

Serves 6.

CHAIR DE CRABES SAUTEE AUX CHAMPIGNONS
Crabmeat Sauteed with Mushrooms

1½ cups butter
2 cups sliced raw mushrooms

5 cups crabmeat
salt and ground white pepper

Put the butter in a large saute pan and heat until fairly hot. Add the mushrooms, cook for one minute, then add the crabmeat. Season with salt and pepper. Continue cooking for only 2 minutes more and serve.

Serves 6.

CHAIR DE CRABES MARINIERE
Crabmeat Mariniere

3 tablespoons butter
1½ cups chopped green onions
1 cup white wine
5 cups lump crabmeat

6 egg yolks
2½ cups warm Bechamel Sauce, page 123
salt, ground white pepper and cayenne

    Saute the green onions in the butter until they become limp. Add the wine and bring to a boil; add the crabmeat and heat in the wine for a few minutes.

    Blend the egg yolks into the Bechamel Sauce and add this to the crabmeat. Season to taste with salt and pepper and cayenne. Cook for a few minutes more without boiling.

Serves 6.

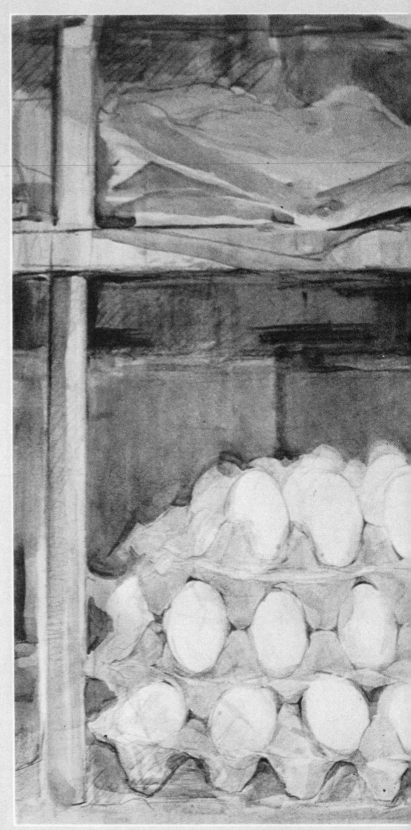

Egg dishes and omelettes
have since the very beginning
been standards of the
Antoine's menu.

OEUFS
Eggs and Omelettes

There have been times in Antoine's past when egg dishes and omelettes were of the most popular dishes served. This goes back to the early years of the operation when the guests of the pension were served petit dejeuner or breakfast and even later when the performers and theatregoers alike would come for a late supper or early breakfast after the theatre closed.

Antoine and Jules created many of the egg dishes which are today standard restaurant fare.

OEUFS BENEDICT
Eggs Benedict

2 slices toast, trimmed of crust
2 teaspoons anchovy paste
2 slices cooked ham (same size as toast)

2 hot poached eggs
½ cup Hollandaise Sauce, page 119
2 slices truffle

Spread each slice of toast with a teaspoon of anchovy paste. Place the toasts on a serving plate and top each with a slice of ham, then a poached egg. Pour ⅓ cup of Hollandaise Sauce over the two eggs and garnish each with a slice of truffle.

Serves 1.

This dish was created by Antoine on the occasion of a dinner he hosted for the French Playwright Victorien Sardou.

EGGS SARDOU

2 warm cooked artichoke hearts	⅓ cup Hollandaise Sauce, page 119
4 anchovy fillets	1 tablespoon chopped ham
2 hot poached eggs	2 slices truffle

Place the hot artichoke hearts on a serving dish. Criss-cross two anchovy fillets over each. Put a poached egg on each artichoke heart. Pour ⅓ cup Hollandaise Sauce over the two eggs. Sprinkle the chopped ham over the two eggs and garnish each with a truffle slice.

Serves 1.

OEUFS ST. DENIS
Eggs St. Denis

2 tablespoons butter	2 slices grilled ham
1 slice white bread	½ cup St. Denis Sauce
2 eggs	

Heat the butter in a small skillet. Trim the bread of crusts and cut in half diagonally. Fry the bread in the hot butter until golden on both sides. Set aside.

French-fry the eggs in deep fat. This is done in almost the same manner as to poach eggs, but the eggs, once they are slipped into the oil, must be turned over continually and very carefully to form an even oval shape. Cook the eggs until the white is firm but the yolk is soft. Remove the eggs from the oil and drain on absorbent paper.

Place the two fried toasts, or croutons, on a serving plate and top each with a slice of grilled ham. Put a fried egg on each slice of ham and cover the two eggs with St. Denis Sauce.

Serves 1.

ST. DENIS SAUCE

1 cup finely chopped chicken livers	¼ teaspoon thyme
⅓ cup finely chopped ham	½ cup sherry
½ cup finely chopped white onions	2 cups Chicken Veloute Sauce, page 123
2 cloves garlic, minced	salt and ground white pepper
3 tablespoons butter	

Blend the chicken livers, ham, onions and garlic together. Saute the mixture in the butter until the onions are limp. Add the thyme and sherry and bring to a boil. Add the Chicken Veloute Sauce and season to taste. Simmer for 20 minutes.

Makes 3 cups.

OEUFS A LA FLORENTINE
Eggs Florentine

½ cup hot Creamed Spinach, page 137   1 teaspoon grated Swiss cheese
2 hot poached eggs   1 teaspoon grated Romano cheese
⅓ cup warm Hollandaise Sauce page 119   1 teaspoon grated Mozzarella cheese
1 tablespoon bread crumbs

Pour the creamed spinach into the bottom of an ovenproof dish and top with the two poached eggs. Cover the eggs with the Hollandaise Sauce. Mix the grated cheeses and breadcrumbs together and sprinkle over the top. Place the dish under the broiler for about 2 minutes or until cheese is melted and top begins to brown.

Serves 1.

OEUFS AUX TOMATES ST. ANTOINE
Eggs St. Antoine

½ cup hot Creole Sauce, page 124
1 slice toast, trimmed of crust
2 hot poached eggs

Force the Creole Sauce through a strainer and keep warm. Put the slice of toast in the bottom of dish and top with the two poached eggs. Cover with the hot Creole Sauce and serve.

Serves 1.

OMELETTES
Omelettes

Almost all of our omelettes are done in the classic French style. Since simplicity is often the reason that many dishes are so delectable, we have tried to remain as simple and as close to the classic preparation as possible. Our only variation from the French omelette is the *Omelette Espagnole*. This omelette is done in the Italian style, which differs from French style in that the ingredients are actually mixed into the eggs and the omelette is cooked and served without folding.

We list only five omelettes on our menu but the variations that we actually serve are endless. We generally leave the combinations and creativity to the individual.

OMELETTE NATURE
Plain Omelette

3 eggs
½ teaspoon salt
dash ground white pepper

2 tablespoons butter
½ teaspoon chopped parsley

Beat the eggs together with the salt and pepper just enough to blend the yolks and whites. Melt the butter in an omelette pan. When hot, add the egg mixture. As the bottom cooks, lift the omelette a bit with a fork to allow the remaining liquid to flow into the bottom of the pan. Loosen the omelette from the pan and fold it into thirds. Cook a short while longer.

Turn the omelette onto a plate, folded side on bottom. Sprinkle with chopped parsley and serve.

Serves 1.

OMELETTE AU FROMAGE
Cheese Omelette

3 eggs
½ teaspoon salt
dash ground white pepper
2 tablespoons butter

2 tablespoons grated Swiss cheese
2 tablespoons grated American cheese
2 tablespoons grated Cheddar cheese
2 tablespoons grated Romano cheese

Prepare the same as the Omelette Nature, but mix the grated cheeses and sprinkle over the omelette before folding into thirds.

Serves 1.

OMELETTE AUX CREVETTES
Shrimp Omelette

3 eggs
½ teaspoon salt
¼ teaspoon ground white pepper

2 tablespoons butter
½ cup peeled, boiled shrimp, page 38

The preparation is the same as Omelette Nature, but spread the shrimp over the omelette before folding.

Serves 1.

OMELETTE A LA CHAIR DE CRABES
Crabmeat Omelette

3 eggs
½ teaspoon salt
¼ teaspoon ground white pepper

2 tablespoons butter
½ cup good lump crabmeat

Again we are using the same preparation as Omelette Nature but spreading the crabmeat over the omelette before folding.

Serves 1.

OMELETTE ESPAGNOLE
Spanish Omelette

1 tablespoon butter
⅓ cup sliced raw mushrooms
⅓ cup cooked green peas
3 eggs

1 teaspoon salt
¼ teaspoon ground white pepper
2 tablespoons butter
½ cup warm Creole Sauce, page 124

Heat the butter in a small pan and quickly saute the sliced mushrooms. Set aside. In a mixing bowl beat the eggs together with the salt and pepper. Mix in the mushrooms and green peas.

Heat the 2 tablespoons of butter in an 8-inch omelette pan and pour in the egg mixture. Cook on a low fire until the omelette has cooked all the way through. Turn out onto a heated serving plate so that the pan side is up. Pour ½ cup of Creole Sauce over the top of the omelette and serve.

Serves 1.

VOLAILLE
Poultry

Waiter John Ketry began working at Antoine's in 1937. His wife, Nancy Ketry, is the office manager and has been at Antoine's since 1946. The strange object on their table is a very old ''duck press,'' sometimes used in the preparation of special menus for private parties.

When Antoine Alciatore first opened the doors of his small
pension *on Rue St. Louis, he served a creation called* Dinde
Talleyrand *or Turkey Talleyrand.*

*This dish has long since disappeared from our menu, but was the
beginning of a procession of dishes that would make his
establishment world famous.*

*The turkey has been replaced principally by chicken, which we
prepare in a good number of delectable ways.*

POULET AUX CHAMPIGNONS
Chicken with Mushrooms

3 chickens, 2½ pounds each
salt and ground white pepper
3 cups raw mushrooms, washed

1½ cups butter
6 sprigs parsley

Wash the chickens and place them in a shallow baking pan. Sprinkle with a little salt and bake in a preheated 350 °F oven for about 1½ hours or until the chickens are fully cooked. Remove from the oven and let the chickens cool. Split the chickens in half and carefully remove and discard the bones.

Halve or quarter the mushrooms, depending on their size, and saute quickly in a pan with 1 cup of hot melted butter. While sauteing the mushrooms season them with a little salt and ground white pepper.

To serve, reheat the boned chicken halves in a large pan with ½ cup butter and then place on a serving plate. Pour the butter from this pan into the mushrooms. Spoon the mushrooms and butter over the chickens. Garnish with a sprig of parsley.

Serves 6.

POULET SAUTE DEMI-BORDELAISE
Chicken Sauteed Demi-Bordelaise

3 chickens, 2½ pounds each
salt and ground white pepper
1½ cups butter

¾ cup chopped garlic
½ cup chopped parsley

Wash and dry the chickens and cut into pieces. Rub the pieces with salt and pepper. Heat the butter and saute the chicken pieces until almost completely cooked. Add the chopped garlic and parsley. Saute for 5 minutes more and serve.

Serves 6.

POULET A LA CREOLE
Chicken Creole

3 chickens, 2½ pounds each
salt and ground white pepper
1 cup olive oil

3 cups Creole Sauce, page 124
3 cups hot cooked rice

Wash and dry the chickens and cut into pieces. Rub the pieces with salt and pepper and brown in hot olive oil. Set aside to drain on absorbent paper.

Put the chicken in a casserole with 3 cups Creole Sauce and simmer very gently for 40 minutes or until chicken is tender. Serve the chicken and sauce with ½ cup cooked rice on each plate.

Serves 6.

POULET AU VIN ROUGE
Chicken in Red Wine Sauce

3 chickens, 2½ pounds each
salt and ground white pepper
flour

1 cup bacon drippings
4 cups Red Wine Sauce

Wash and dry the chickens and cut into pieces. Rub the pieces with salt and pepper and dredge in flour. Heat the bacon drippings and brown the chicken.

Put the chicken in a large casserole and add the Red Wine Sauce. Cover and simmer for about 40 minutes or until chicken is tender. Adjust the seasoning if necessary.

Serves 6.

RED WINE SAUCE

½ pound bacon cut in julienne strips
2 cups chopped white onions
1½ cups red wine
2 cloves garlic, minced
1 small stalk celery

2 bay leaves
2 sprigs parsley
3 cups Espagnole Sauce, page 126
salt and ground white pepper

Put the bacon in a saucepan and cook until almost crisp. Remove the bacon and set aside. Add the onions to the pan with the bacon grease and saute until golden. Add the red wine and bring to a boil.

Add the garlic, celery, bay leaves, parsley and Espagnole Sauce. Season to taste and simmer for 20 minutes. Strain the sauce. Add the bacon to the sauce and keep warm.

Makes 4 cups.

POULET SAUCE ROCHAMBEAU
Chicken Rochambeau

3 chickens, 2½ pounds each
salt and ground white pepper
1 stick butter

6 slices cooked ham
2 cups Brown Rochambeau Sauce
2 cups Bearnaise Sauce, page 119

Wash and dry the chickens and rub inside and out with salt, pepper and butter. Put them in a shallow baking pan and into a preheated 350 °F. oven for 1½ hours or until completely cooked. Split the chickens in half and remove the bones and return to a low oven to keep warm.

Put the ham slices in a saucepan with the Brown Rochambeau Sauce and simmer for a few minutes.

Put a slice of ham on each plate and spoon on some of the brown sauce. Top the ham with ½ boned chicken and cover the chicken with Bearnaise sauce.

Serves 6.

BROWN ROCHAMBEAU SAUCE

3 tablespoons butter
1 cup chopped onions
3 tablespoons flour
⅓ cup vinegar

2 tablespoons sugar
2 cups chicken stock, page 115
salt and ground white pepper

Saute the chopped onions in the butter until they begin to color. Add 3 tablespoons flour and cook until brown. Blend in the vinegar, then the sugar.

Add the chicken stock and season to taste with salt and pepper. Simmer for 20 minutes.

Makes 2½ cups.

POULET A LA PARISIENNE
Parisian Chicken

3 chickens, 2½ pounds each
1½ cups half and half
3 eggs
2 teaspoons salt
1 teaspoon ground white pepper

1½ cups flour
2 cups breadcrumbs
2 cups Bearnaise Sauce, page 119
3 cups French-style green peas, page 137

Wash and dry the chickens and split them in half. Remove and discard the breast bones.

Make a batter by combining the half and half, eggs, salt and pepper. Dredge the chicken halves in flour, then dip in the batter, then roll in breadcrumbs. Fry in deep fat until golden brown and completely cooked. Drain on absorbent paper.

Served topped with Bearnaise Sauce, with ½ cup green peas on the same plate.

Serves 6.

POULET BONNE FEMME
Chicken Bonne Femme

1 pound bacon cut in julienne strips
3 large potatoes
3 chickens, 2½ pounds each
salt and ground white pepper

1 cup butter
2 cups chopped onion
3 cloves garlic, minced

Cook the bacon until almost crisp and remove from the skillet, leaving the drippings. Wash and peel the potatoes and cut them into 1/8 inch slices, like potato chips. Saute these potatoes in the hot bacon drippings until they are limp. Keep warm.

Wash and dry the chickens, disjoint them and season with salt and pepper. Saute the pieces in a pan with 1 cup butter until the chicken is nice and brown. Add the onions and cook until they become limp. Add the garlic.

Combine the bacon and the potatoes with the chicken and adjust the seasoning. Cook together for 10 minutes more.

Serves 6.

PIGEONNEAUX PARADIS
Squabs with Paradise Sauce

6 squabs
salt and ground white pepper

½ stick butter
3 cups Paradise Sauce

Wash and dry the squabs. Rub inside and out with salt, pepper and butter. Place in a shallow baking pan and cook in a preheated 325 °F. oven for about 45 minutes or until done. Place the squabs in a deep casserole with 3 cups Paradise Sauce and simmer gently for 20 minutes.

Serves 6.

PARADISE SAUCE

⅓ pound bacon cut in julienne strips
¾ cup green onions cut in julienne strips
¾ cup celery cut in julienne strips
3 tablespoons butter
3 tablespoons currant jelly

1 cup canned seedless white grapes
½ cup of juice in which the grapes are
  packed
1 cup thick Chicken Veloute Sauce, page 123

Fry the bacon, discard the grease and set aside. Saute the celery and onions in the butter until limp. Add the bacon, currant jelly and the juice from the grapes. Bring to a boil, add the Veloute Sauce and the grapes. Simmer for 45 minutes.

Makes 3 cups.

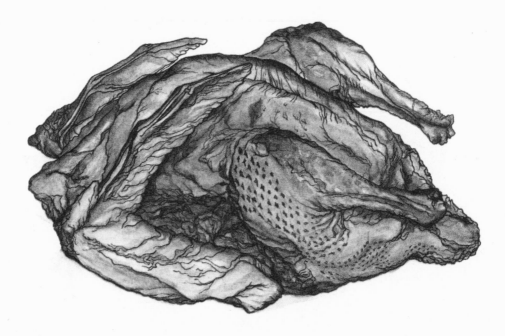

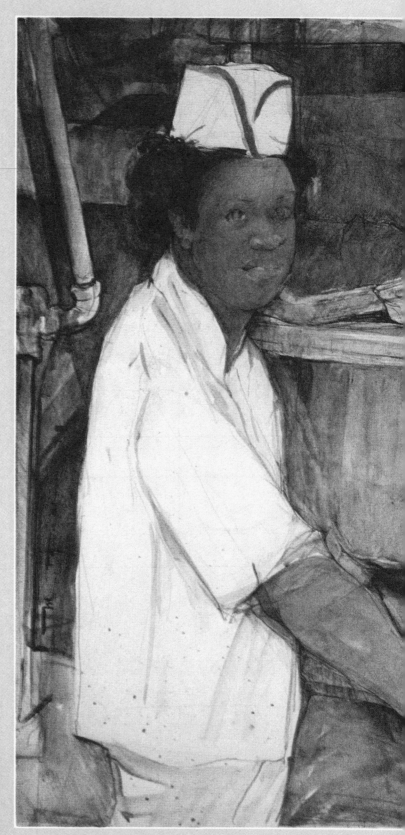

Johnnie Hankton, assistant
night chef, stands at the grill
where the meats are cooked.
Antoine's serves the best meat
available in the United States
and perhaps the world.

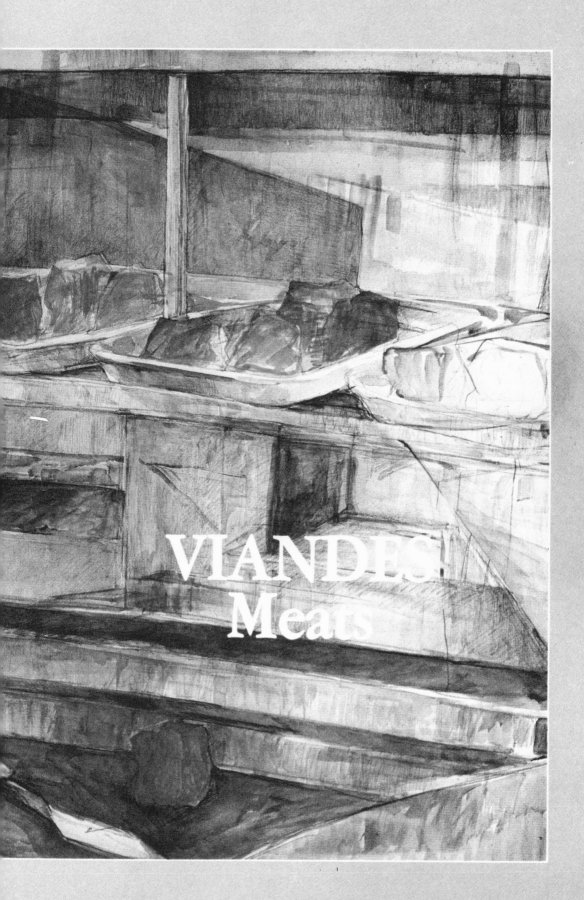

VIANDES
Meats

Antoine's has used the best products available to produce the fine cuisine here.

Our meat is the finest available in the United States and possibly the world. And our sauces to accompany the meat dishes are some of the best produced anywhere.

COTELETTES D'AGNEAU GRILLEES
Grilled Lamb Chops

2 double lamb chops, 7 ounces each
oil
salt

2 tablespoons hot melted butter
1 teaspoon chopped parsley
mint jelly

Brush the lamb chops with oil and salt lightly. Cook the chops on a grill or in a heavy iron skillet to desired doneness. First on one side, then the other side. Remove to serving dish and pour over the melted butter and some chopped parsley. Serve with mint jelly on the side.

Serves 1.

NOISETTES D'AGNEAU MAISON D'OR
Hearts of Lamb Chops with Maison d'Or Sauce

2 double lamb chops, 7 ounces each
1 strip bacon
oil

salt
⅓ cup Maison d'Or Sauce, page 124

Cut the hearts from the chops and place them together side by side. Wrap them with a strip of bacon and pierce with a metal skewer to hold together. Brush with oil, salt lightly and cook on a grill or heavy iron skillet to desired doneness.

Remove the skewer and top with ⅓ cup Maison d'Or Sauce.

Serves 1.

107

RIS DE VEAU A LA FINANCIERE
Sweetbreads with Financiere Sauce

2½ pounds veal sweetbreads
salt and ground white pepper

⅓ cup melted butter
3 cups Financiere Sauce, page 129

Boil the sweetbreads in water for a minute or two. Remove from the water, drain and put them in a shallow baking pan. Sprinkle with salt and pepper and ⅓ cup melted butter. Place in a preheated 375 °F oven for about 15 minutes or until they begin to color.

Remove from the oven and cut into 1-inch pieces. Put the pieces into a saucepan with 3 cups Financiere Sauce. Cook without boiling for 15 minutes more.

Serves 6.

ENTRECOTE NATURE
Grilled Sirloin Steak

1 sirloin steak, 12 ounces
oil
salt

1 slice of toast, trimmed of crust
2 tablespoons melted butter
½ teaspoon chopped parsley

Brush the sirloin with oil and season lightly with salt. Cook on a grill or heavy iron skillet, first one side then the other, to desired doneness. To serve, place the steak on the toast and pour the melted butter over it. Sprinkle with chopped parsley.

Or, serve with ⅓ cup of any of the following sauces: Alciatore, Marchand de Vin, Bearnaise, Medicis, Maison D'Or, Financiere, Robespierre, Champignons or Demi-Bordelaise.

Serves 1.

TOURNEDOS NATURE
Grilled Small Filet

Use a 6½ ounce filet of beef. Prepare the same way as the Entrecote Nature and serve with any of the same accompanying sauces.

FILET DE BOEUF NATURE
Grilled Filet

Use a 9½ ounce filet of beef and prepare the same as the Entrecote Nature using any of the same accompanying sauces.

TIPS DE FILET EN BROCHETTE MEDICIS
Filet Tips with Medicis Sauce

4 pieces of filet tips,	oil
2 inches square	salt
3 pieces bacon, 2 inches long	1 slice toast, trimmed of crust
1 skewer	⅓ cup Medicis Sauce, page 127

The filet tips come from the end of the tenderloin and are too small to be used for filets. Push the filet tips, with a piece of bacon in between each, onto the skewer. Brush with oil and season with salt. Cook on a grill to desired doneness.

Put the toast on the plate, and the filet tips on the toast. Remove the skewer. Pour the Medicis Sauce over the tips and serve.

Serves 1.

CHATEAUBRIAND
Double Filet with Colbert Sauce

1 center-cut filet, 20 ounces	1 large potato
oil	4 tablespoons butter
salt	⅔ cup Colbert Sauce, page 120

Brush the meat with oil and sprinkle with salt. Cook to desired doneness on a grill or in a heavy iron skillet.

Meanwhile wash and peel the potato and cut into 4 or 6 pieces as for fried potatoes. Saute in the butter until golden brown and keep warm.

Put the Chateaubriand onto a serving dish and surround with the cooked potatoes. Cover the meat with the Colbert Sauce and bring to the table. At the table cut the meat into four slices. Serve each person 2 slices with some potatoes and Colbert Sauce.

Serves 2.

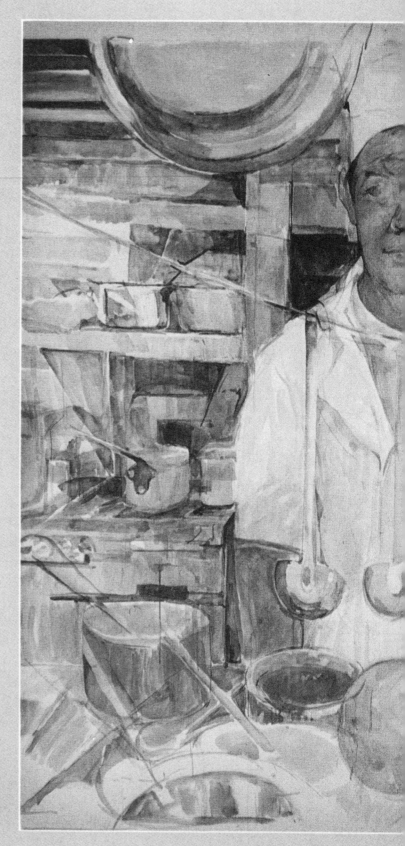

Chef John DeVille, at Antoine's for 15 years, shown here with the sauces — often the most difficult and most important part of Antoine's dishes.

SAUCES
Sauces

The sauce is the lifeblood of our cuisine. It contains the elements needed to produce dishes which have taken generations to develop.

The sauce is often the most difficult and most important part of any dish. Prepare it carefully.

Not included in this section are sauces which are used only once; those I have placed with the recipe for that particular dish.

FISH STOCK

10 pounds fish heads and bones
3 onions sliced
2 stalks celery
2 bay leaves

3 sprigs parsley
2 tablespoons salt
3 quarts water

Add all ingredients, including the water, to a large soup pot. Simmer for 4 hours skimming the scum off the top from time to time. Strain.

Makes 2 quarts.

CHICKEN STOCK

10 pounds chicken scraps and bones
3 onions, sliced
3 carrots, sliced
2 stalks celery
1 bell pepper, quartered

2 bay leaves
3 sprigs parsley
2 tablespoons salt
3 quarts water

Add all ingredients including the water to a large soup pot. Simmer for 4 hours skimming the fat off the top from time to time. Strain.

Makes 2 quarts.

BEEF STOCK

1 stick butter
4 pounds beef scraps or soup meat
8 pounds beef and veal bones
3 peeled onions, sliced
3 carrots, sliced
2 stalks celery

1 bell pepper, quartered
2 bay leaves
3 sprigs parsley
2 tablespoons salt
3 quarts water

Melt the butter in a large soup pot and brown the meat and bones with the onions. Add all remaining ingredients.

Simmer for 4 hours, skimming the fat off the top from time to time. Strain.

Makes 2 quarts.

VINAIGRETTE SAUCE

½ teaspoon salt
¼ teaspoon finely ground white pepper
½ teaspoon dry powdered mustard

⅓ cup vinegar
1 cup olive oil

Put all ingredients into a bottle and shake to mix. Store at room temperature.

Makes 1½ cups.

COCKTAIL SAUCE

4 tablespoons horseradish
3 tablespoons worcestershire
1 tablespoon Tobasco sauce

½ cup Vinaigrette Sauce
2 cups ketchup
¼ cup lemon juice

Blend all ingredients together and chill.

Makes 3 cups.

MAYONNAISE
Mayonnaise

3 eggs yolks
¾ teaspoon salt
¼ teaspoon ground white pepper

2½ tablespoons tarragon vinegar
1¼ cup oil

Beat the egg yolks together with the salt, pepper and half of the vinegar. Continue beating and add half of the oil a little at a time. Add the rest of the vinegar, and continue beating while you gradually add the remainder of the oil. Chill.

Makes 1½ cups.

DEMI-BORDELAISE SAUCE

2 sticks butter
2 cups chopped garlic
¼ cup chopped parsley

Melt the butter and saute the garlic for a brief moment. Add the parsley and serve.

Makes 1½ cups.

BOURGUIGNONNE SAUCE

1 cup finely minced parsley
1 cup finely minced green onions
½ cup finely minced garlic

2 sticks softened butter
1 teaspoon salt

Blend all the ingredients together well. Keep at a cool temperature.

Makes 3½ cups.

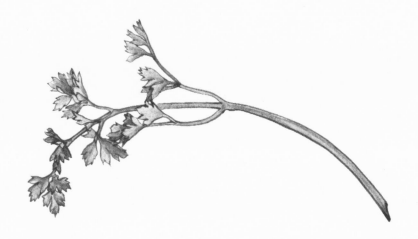

HOLLANDAISE SAUCE

2 cups melted butter, warm
8 egg yolks
2 tablespoons lemon juice

2 tablespoons tarragon vinegar
¾ teaspoon paprika
salt and cayenne pepper to taste

Beat the egg yolks together with the lemon juice and vinegar and pour the mixture into the top of a double boiler. Cook on a low heat stirring constantly, never letting the water in the double boiler come to a boil. Continue cooking until the mixture thickens. Remove from the fire and beat in the warm melted butter, a little at a time. Add the paprika and salt and pepper. Keep warm but not hot.

Makes 2 cups.

BEARNAISE SAUCE

¼ cup minced white onion
2 tablespoons minced tarragon leaves
¼ cup tarragon vinegar

2 tablespoons chopped parsley
1 ¾ cups warm Hollandaise Sauce

Put the onion, tarragon leaves and tarragon vinegar in a pot and reduce the liquid completely.
Cool slightly and blend in the Hollandaise Sauce.

Makes 1¾ cups.

COLBERT SAUCE

⅔ cups Tomato Sauce, page 125
⅓ cup sherry
¾ cup warm Hollandaise Sauce, page 119
caramel food color

Put the Tomato Sauce and the sherry in a saucepan and reduce to ⅔ cup. Let cool slightly and blend with the Hollandaise. Add enough caramel color to give the sauce a nice brown color. Keep warm.

Makes 1½ cups.

ALCIATORE SAUCE

1 slice pineapple, hot
⅓ cup Brown Pineapple Sauce,
  below

⅓ cup Bearnaise Sauce, page 119
1 mushroom top, sauteed in
  1 teaspoon butter

Heat the pineapple slice in the Brown Pineapple Sauce. Place the slice of pineapple on a hot serving plate and top with the Brown Pineapple Sauce.

Now put the cooked meat (any cut may be used) on the pineapple slice and top with the Bearnaise Sauce and whole sauteed mushroom top.

Serves 1.

BROWN PINEAPPLE SAUCE

⅓ cup sugar
⅓ cup water
2 cups pineapple juice
⅓ cup vinegar

⅓ cup sherry
3 tablespoons butter
3 tablespoons flour

In a saucepan, caramelize the sugar with the water and then add the pineapple juice, vinegar and sherry. Cook at a boil until the liquid is reduced by ⅓.

In a small skillet, melt the butter and blend in the flour. Cook together, stirring constantly, until it becomes a rich brown color. Blend this into the sauce.

Simmer gently for 20 minutes.

Makes 2 cups.

BECHAMEL SAUCE

2 tablespoons butter
2 tablespoons flour

1½ cups warm scalded milk
salt and ground white pepper

Melt the butter and stir in the flour. Stir and cook without coloring until mixture becomes foamy. Stir in the milk and bring to a boil, then turn fire down to a simmer. Add salt and pepper to taste. Remove from the fire and dot top of sauce with a few pieces of butter to prevent a film from forming.

Makes 1½ cups.

VELOUTE SAUCE

2 tablespoons butter
2 tablespoons flour
salt and ground white pepper

1½ cups warm Fish or Chicken Stock, page 115

Melt the butter and stir in the flour. Stir and cook until the mixture becomes foamy. Add the warm stock and bring to a boil. Turn fire down to a simmer and add salt and pepper to taste. Remove from the fire and dot top of sauce with a few pieces of butter to prevent a film from forming.

Makes 1½ cups.

MAISON D'OR SAUCE

⅓ cup raw sweetbreads
2 tablespoons melted butter
⅓ cup raw sliced mushrooms
⅓ cup cooked turkey breast,
   cut into ½ inch cubes

½ truffle, chopped
½ cup sherry
½ cup Bechamel Sauce, page 123
salt and pepper to taste

Boil the sweetbreads in water, drain, then put them in a shallow baking pan. Sprinkle with 1 tablespoon melted butter and a dash of salt and pepper and place the pan in a 375 °F oven. Brown slightly and remove from the oven. Chop them up.

Saute the mushrooms in the remaining tablespoon of butter until they become limp. Add the chopped sweetbreads, turkey and truffle. Cook together for a few minutes then add the sherry. Bring to a boil and add the Bechamel Sauce. Season to taste and cook at a gentle simmer for a few minutes more.

Makes 1½ cups.

CREOLE SAUCE

2 tablespoons butter
1 cup chopped bell pepper
1 cup chopped onion
3 cups chopped tomato pulp
¼ teaspoon dried thyme
2 bay leaves

4 cloves garlic, minced
2 tablespoons parsley, minced
1 teaspoon paprika
salt and cayenne pepper to taste
1 tablespoon cornstarch

Melt the butter and saute the onions and bell pepper until they become limp. Add all the remaining ingredients except the cornstarch, and season to taste with salt and cayenne pepper. Simmer for 20 minutes.

Mix the cornstarch with a little water and blend in to the sauce. Cook for a few minutes more to thicken.

Makes 3 cups.

TOMATO SAUCE

3 tablespoons butter
¾ cup chopped onion
2 tablespoons flour
2 cups Chicken Stock, page 115
1½ cups chopped tomato pulp
¼ teaspoon dried thyme

2 cloves garlic, minced
½ stalk celery, chopped
2 sprigs parsley, chopped
1 bay leaf
salt and ground white pepper

Melt 2 tablespoons of the butter in a saucepan and add the chopped onion. Cook until they begin to color, add the remaining tablespoon butter, the flour and cook until golden brown. Stir often to be sure nothing sticks to the pan. Now add all remaining ingredients and season to taste. Simmer for 30 minutes. Pass sauce through a strainer.

Makes 2 cups.

ESPAGNOLE SAUCE

3 tablespoons butter
½ cup finely chopped onion
½ cup finely chopped carrot
3 tablespoons flour
3 cups Beef or Chicken Stock, page 115
1 cup Tomato Sauce, page 125
2 cloves garlic, minced
½ teaspoon dried thyme

1 small stalk celery
2 bay leaves
3 sprigs parsley
1 teaspoon sugar
1 teaspoon water
3 tablespoons vinegar
¼ teaspoon anchovy paste
salt and ground white pepper

Melt 2 tablespoons of butter in a saucepan and cook the onion and carrot until they begin to color. Add the remaining tablespoon butter, stir in the flour and cook until brown. Add the stock, tomato sauce, garlic, thyme, celery, bay and parsley.

In a small saucepan, caramelize 1 teaspoon sugar with 1 teaspoon water; remove from heat and immediately add the vinegar. Mix in the anchovy paste and add this mixture to the Espagnole Sauce. Salt and pepper to taste, bring to a boil and simmer for 30 minutes. Strain.

Makes 2 cups.

MARCHAND DE VIN SAUCE

2 tablespoons butter
1 cup chopped onions
1 cup chopped mushrooms
6 cloves garlic, minced

1 cup red wine
2 cups Espagnole Sauce
salt and pepper

Puree the onions, mushrooms and garlic and cook together with the butter in a saucepan until they become a light brown color. Add the Espagnole Sauce, salt and pepper to taste, and simmer for 30 minutes.

Makes 3 cups.

MEDICIS SAUCE

2 tablespoons butter
1 cup minced bell pepper
⅔ cup sherry

2 cups Espagnole Sauce, opposite page
salt and pepper to taste

Saute the bell pepper in the butter until it becomes limp. Add the sherry and bring to a boil. Add the Espagnole Sauce, salt and pepper, and simmer for 30 minutes.

Makes 2 cups.

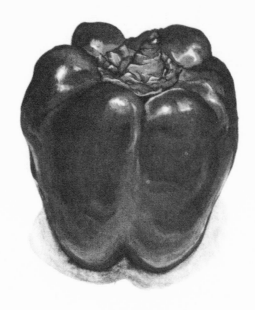

CHAMPIGNON SAUCE

2 tablespoons butter
3 cups sliced mushrooms
½ cup red wine

1½ cups Espagnole Sauce, page 126
salt and pepper

Saute the mushrooms in butter without coloring. Add red wine. Boil for a minute. Add the Espagnole Sauce and salt and pepper to taste. Simmer for 30 minutes.

Makes 2½ cups.

FINANCIERE SAUCE

2 tablespoons butter
¾ cup chicken livers, cut in halves
⅔ cup pitted green olives
1 cup water
⅓ pound bacon cut in julienne strips

1 cup chopped green onions
½ cup sherry
2 cups Espagnole Sauce, page 126
salt and ground white pepper

Saute the chicken livers in the butter and set aside. In another saucepan put the olives and water and bring to a boil. Remove the olives, cut them into halves and set aside.

Saute the bacon until it is about half cooked then add the green onions and continue cooking until they become limp. Add the sherry and bring to a boil. Now add the Espagnole Sauce, the cooked chicken livers and the olives. Add salt and pepper to taste and simmer for 30 minutes.

Makes 3 cups.

✿

ROBESPIERRE SAUCE

¾ pound veal sweetbreads
1 cup Financiere Sauce, above

This sauce is actually the same as the dish Ris De Veau Financière, differing slightly, in that the sweetbreads and chicken livers are chopped after they are cooked, before adding them to the Financière Sauce, above. See page 108.

Makes about 2½ cups.

Burke Brouillette has been
making Pommes de Terre
Soufflees for nearly all of his 24
years at Antoine's. The oil in
which the potatoes are cooked
bubbles in huge, specially made
black pots. The "baskets" in
which they are served are hand
woven every day from potato
strips.

LEGUMES
Vegetables

The most famous of all of our vegetable dishes is Pommes de Terre Soufflees *or Puffed Potatoes. The story of their creation and the secret of their preparation was given to Antoine by the great chef Collinet, during Antoine's apprenticeship at the Hotel de Noailles in Marseilles.*

The story goes that the occasion was the first run of the railroad from Paris to St. Germain-en-Laye.

Louis Philippe, then king of France, was going to ride the train on its inaugural run to St. Germain-en-Laye, where there would be a great celebration and feast.

Chef Collinet, who was preparing the feast, had a messenger waiting for the train's arrival. As soon as the messenger could see the train approaching, he rushed to Collinet to inform him. The great chef threw his potatoes, which he had cut for frying, into the oil to cook. Louis Philippe had a penchant for fried potatoes and insisted on having them at every meal.

Unfortunately for Collinet, the king was not on the train. The king's advisors had at the last minute forced him to ride in a carriage alongside of the train as they feared for his life on this unproven track.

When Collinet realized that the king was not on the train, he removed the potatoes from the oil and set them aside. What a dilemma! There were no more potatoes to cook and the king would be furious.

So, Collinet waited, and some time later Louis Philippe finally arrived, and the banquet began. Collinet's only choice was to reheat the cooked potatoes. Back into the grease, which had become extremely hot from sitting on the fire, they went, and to the amazement of everyone, they puffed up into small balloon shapes. The king was both thrilled and amazed and showered Collinet with compliments.

Antoine brought the recipe with him to New Orleans and Pommes de Terre Souflees *have been served here ever since.*

POMMES DE TERRE SOUFFLEES
Puffed Potatoes

2 pounds large Idaho potatoes
oil
salt

Wash and peel the potatoes and cut lengthwise into slices 1¼ inches wide and one-eighth inch thick. Soak the potato slices in cold water to remove excess starch.

Have two pots filled with oil, one at a moderately hot temperature (275 °F) and the other at a very hot temperature (400 °F). Drain the potatoes and dry them carefully. Put a single layer of potatoes into a frying basket and lower the basket into the moderately hot oil. Keep moving the potatoes around, dipping the basket in and out of the oil until the potatoes begin to brown and to puff. The partially cooked potatoes may be set aside for awhile before the second stage, or may be finished immediately.

Put the partially cooked potatoes in a basket and dip the basket into the pot of very hot oil. Again be careful to cover only the bottom of the basket with potatoes and to keep them moving around in the oil until they are golden brown, well puffed and crispy.

Remove from the oil, drain on absorbent paper and sprinkle with salt for seasoning.

Serves 6.

Note: Idaho potatoes generally work best. They should be old enough to have become rubbery to the touch and not hard. At this point of ripeness they often begin to bud.

EPINARDS SAUCE CREME
Creamed Spinach

3 pounds raw spinach
2 tablespoons butter

1 cup hot Bechamel Sauce, page 123
salt and ground white pepper

Wash the spinach and break it into pieces discarding the stems. Put the damp leaves into a saucepan with two tablespoons butter. Cover the pot and cook over a moderate heat for ten minutes.

Add the Bechamel Sauce, season to taste, and simmer gently for a few minutes more.

Serves 6.

PETITS POIS A LA FRANCAISE
French-Style Green Peas

⅓ cup chopped ham
3 tablespoons butter
½ cup chopped green onions
½ cup chopped lettuce leaves
1 bay leaf

2½ cups canned baby peas in packing
    water
½ cup additional water
2 tablespoons butter
2 tablespoons flour
salt and ground white pepper

Saute the ham in the butter for a minute then add the green onions, lettuce and bay leaf. Continue cooking until the vegetables are limp. Add the peas and packing water and the extra water. Bring to a boil.

In a skillet melt the butter and add the flour. Stir and cook for two minutes. Blend flour and butter mixture with some of the liquid and add to the peas. Season to taste with salt and pepper. Cook until liquid thickens and serve.

Makes 3 cups.

CHOU-FLEUR AU BEURRE
Cauliflower with Butter

1 large head cauliflower
1 tablespoon salt
1½ cups hot melted butter

Trim the stem and leaves from the cauliflower and put it in a deep casserole. Pour in enough boiling water to cover the cauliflower and add the tablespoon of salt. Cook in the boiling water for 20 to 30 minutes or until the cauliflower is slightly tender all the way through.

Remove from the water and cut into small flowerets. Serve each person about ½ cup of the flowerets with ¼ cup butter poured over.

Serves 6.

CHOU-FLEUR AU GRATIN
Cauliflower au Gratin

1 large head cauliflower
1½ cups Bechamel Sauce, page 123
salt and pepper
3 tablespoons grated Swiss cheese

3 tablespoons grated Romano cheese
3 tablespoons grated Mozzarella cheese
¼ cup breadcrumbs

Cook the cauliflower using the same method as for Chou-Fleur Au Beurre but after boiling the cauliflower, cut into small, one-inch pieces. In a mixing bowl carefully blend the cauliflower pieces with the Bechamel Sauce, season with salt and pepper, if necessary, and spoon into small ovenproof dishes.

Mix the grated cheeses and breadcrumbs together and sprinkle it over the cauliflower mixture. Place in a preheated hot oven, 400 °F, until the cheese is melted and begins to brown.

Serves 6.

CAROTTES AU BEURRE
Carrots with Butter

1 pound carrots   1 cup melted butter
1 tablespoon salt

Wash, scrape and trim the carrots. Put them in a casserole with the tablespoon of salt and enough boiling water to cover. Let the water boil gently until the carrots become slightly tender.

Remove from the water and cut into ½ inch pieces. Serve with melted butter poured over.

Serves 6.

BROCCOLI SAUCE HOLLANDAISE
Broccoli with Hollandaise Sauce

2 pounds broccoli   2 cups Hollandaise Sauce, page 119
1 teaspoon salt

Wash the broccoli well and trim off the hard end of the stem. Cover the bottom of a large saucepan with 2 inches of water. Add the teaspoon of salt and bring to a boil. Place the broccoli in the saucepan, cover and cook until slightly tender.

Remove the broccoli from the saucepan and divide into six portions. Pour ⅓ cup Hollandaise Sauce over each portion and serve.

Serves 6.

ASPERGES AU BEURRE
Asparagus with Butter

2½ pounds asparagus
1 teaspoon salt

1 cup melted butter

Wash the asparagus and cut off the tough end of the stalks. Lay them in the bottom of a wide saucepan and pour in enough boiling water to cover. Add the salt and cover the pan. Continue boiling gently until the asparagus begin to become tender.

Remove from the water, drain and serve with butter poured over.

Serves 6.

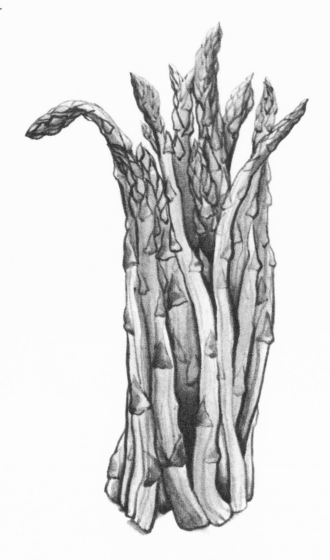

HARICOTS VERTS AU BEURRE
Green Beans with Butter

1 pound green beans   1 cup hot melted butter
1 teaspoon salt

Wash the green beans and break off the tips. Cut into pieces 1½ inches long and put them into a saucepan. Add the teaspoon of salt and enough boiling water to cover. Cover the pan and cook with the water gently boiling until beans are slightly tender.

Remove the beans from the water, drain and serve with melted butter poured over.

Serves 6.

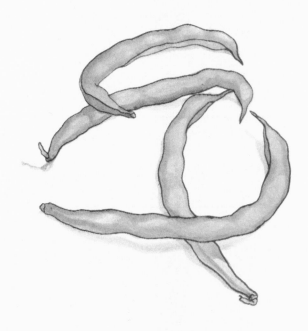

POMMES DE TERRE AU GRATIN
Potatoes Au Gratin

2 pounds potatoes
1 tablespoon salt
2 cups Bechamel Sauce, page 123
3 tablespoons grated Swiss cheese

3 tablespoons grated Romano cheese
3 tablespoons grated Mozzarella cheese
¼ cup breadcrumbs
salt and ground white pepper

Wash and peel the potatoes. Place them in the bottom of a large saucepan and add enough boiling water to cover. Add one tablespoon of salt, cover the pan and continue boiling the potatoes until they are tender when pierced with a sharp knife. Remove the potatoes from the water and cut into ½ inch cubes.

Combine the potato cubes with the Bechamel Sauce, being careful not to break them up. Add salt and pepper if needed.

Spoon the potato mixture into six small individual ovenproof dishes. Mix the cheeses and the breadcrumbs and sprinkle on top. Place in a hot preheated 400 °F oven until the cheese is melted and the top begins to brown.

Serves 6.

POMMES DE TERRE BRABANT
Sauteed Potatoes

2 pounds potatoes
1 cup butter

1 teaspoon salt
¼ cup chopped parsley

Wash and peel the potatoes. Cut them into ¾ inch cubes and saute them in the butter until golden brown.

Season with salt and serve with the cooking butter poured over. Sprinkle with chopped parsley.

Serves 6.

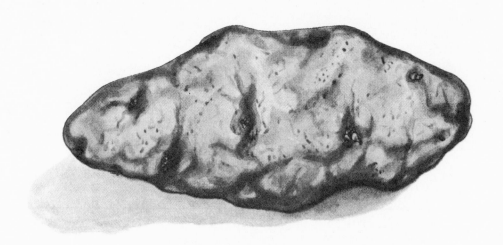

Eddie Adams has been at
Antoine's for 12 years. He is
shown here in the pantry section
of Antoine's kitchen.

SALADES
Salads

*An interesting and diversified collection, our salads offer
something to please even the most particular palate.*

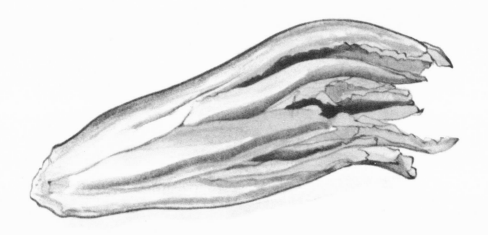

SALADE ANTOINE
Antoine Salad

1 bunch watercress
2 Belgian endive
1 small head bibb lettuce

1 small head romaine
1 cup Vinaigrette Sauce, page 117

Wash and dry all the greens. Remove the stems and undesirable parts and break the leaves into two-inch pieces. Toss the greens together and chill, covered, in the refrigerator.

Just before serving toss the salad lightly with the Vinaigrette Sauce.

Serves 6.

SALADE D'ANCHOIS
Anchovy Salad

Prepare in the same way, using the same ingredients, as Salade Antoine, but chop up about 2½ dozen anchovy fillets and toss into the salad with the Vinaigrette Sauce. See Salade Antoine, above.

Serves 6.

SALADE DE LAITUE ET TOMATES
Lettuce and Tomato Salad

1 large head bibb lettuce
3 large tomatoes
1½ cups Vinaigrette Sauce, page 117

Wash and dry the head of lettuce without taking it apart. Cut the lettuce into six equal horizontal slices.

Wash and dry the tomatoes, remove the stems and cut into four horizontal slices. Cut each slice in half.

Put a slice of lettuce on each chilled salad plate. Surround each lettuce slice with four half slices of tomato. Pour ¼ cup Vinaigrette Sauce over each salad.

Serves 6.

SALADE DE LAITUE AU ROQUEFORT
Lettuce Salad with Roquefort Dressing

1 large head bibb lettuce
2 cups Roquefort Dressing, below

Wash and dry the lettuce, leaving the head intact. Cut the head all the way across into six equal slices.

Place each slice of lettuce on a chilled salad plate and cover with ⅓ cup Roquefort Dressing.

Serves 6.

ROQUEFORT DRESSING

⅔ cup crumbled Roquefort cheese
1⅓ cups Vinaigrette Sauce, page 117

Blend the crumbled Roquefort cheese with the Vinaigrette Sauce. Chill.

Makes 2 cups.

SALADE DE LEGUMES
Vegetable Salad

2 cups cooked cauliflower
2 cups cooked carrots
2 cups cooked broccoli
3 cups shredded lettuce

1½ cups Vinaigrette Sauce, page 117
2 dozen cold cooked asparagus tips
12 tomato slices, halved

Chop the cauliflower, carrots, and broccoli. Toss them together and chill, covered, in the refrigerator.

To serve, put ½ cup shredded lettuce on the bottom of each of six cold salad plates. Toss the vegetables with the Vinaigrette Sauce and put one cup of the mixture on each bed of lettuce. Top each salad with 4 asparagus tips and garnish each plate with 4 half slices of tomato.

Serves 6.

AVOCAT A LA VINAIGRETTE
Avocado with Vinaigrette Sauce

1 ripe avocado, chilled
1 cup chopped lettuce
½ cup Vinaigrette Sauce, page 117

Cut the avocado in half and remove the seed. Put ½ cup chopped lettuce on each of 2 chilled salad plates. Pour ¼ cup Vinaigrette Sauce into and over each avocado.

Serves 2.

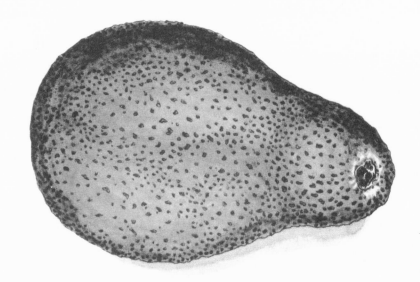

AVOCAT EVANTAIL
Fan Avocado

1 avocado, chilled
1 cup chopped lettuce leaves

4 strips pimento
½ cup Vinaigrette Sauce, page 117

Remove the skin from the avocado and cut in half lengthwise. Put the avocado halves on a cutting surface, cut side down. Slice them lengthwise with vertical cuts, ¼ inch apart.

Put ½ cup chopped lettuce on each of two chilled salad plates. Take the avocado halves and spread them out as you would a fan (*evantail* is French for fan) and place each on one of the prepared plates.

Top each avocado with a cross of 2 pimento strips and cover with ¼ cup Vinaigrette Sauce.

Serves 2.

153

SALADE MIRABEAU
Mirabeau Salad

1 chilled avocado
1 cup chopped lettuce leaves

2 tomato slices, halved
½ cup Thousand Island Dressing

Put ½ cup chopped lettuce on each of 2 chilled salad plates. Halve the avocado and remove the seed. Scoop out the meat of the avocado with a teaspoon or small melon ball scoop to form balls. Put the balls of meat on the prepared salad plates and garnish each plate with two half slices of tomato.

Top each salad with ¼ cup Thousand Island Dressing.

Serves 2.

THOUSAND ISLAND DRESSING

1½ cups Mayonnaise, page 117
½ cup ketchup

Blend the Mayonnaise and the ketchup and store in the refrigerator.

Makes 2 cups.

FONDS D'ARTICHAUTS BAYARD
Hearts of Artichoke Bayard

6 cooked artichokes
1 cup minced celery
1 cup minced parsley
1 cup minced green onion
1½ dozen anchovy fillets
1 teaspoon salt

½ teaspoon ground white pepper
3 cups chopped lettuce
6 slices tomato, halved
1 hard-boiled egg, chopped
3 teaspoons caviar
1½ cups Vinaigrette Sauce, page 117

Scrape the meat from the leaves of the cooked artichokes. Retain the meat and the hearts and discard the rest. Mince a dozen of the anchovy fillets and mix together with the celery, parsley, green onions, salt, pepper and the meat scrapings. Form the mixture into six balls, equal in size, and squeeze out the excess moisture.

Cover each of the six chilled salad plates with ½ cup chopped lettuce. Place an artichoke heart in the center of each plate and top each with a ball of the minced vegetable mixture. Garnish each with two halves of a slice of tomato. Chill.

To serve, pour ¼ cup Vinaigrette Sauce over the top of each Bayard and sprinkle with chopped egg. Top with one anchovy fillet formed into a ring and filled with ½ teaspoon caviar.

Serves 6.

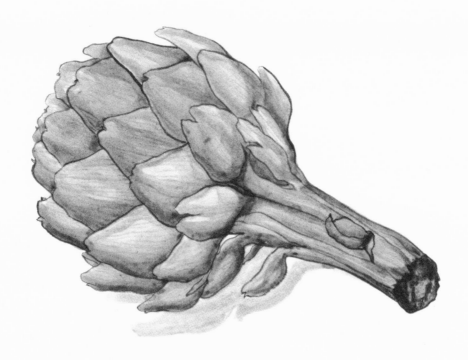

SALADE DE COUERS DE PALMIER
Hearts of Palm Salad

3 cups chopped lettuce leaves
6 slices tomato, halved

3 cups hearts of palm, cut into
1 inch pieces
1½ cups Vinaigrette Sauce, page 117

Put ½ cup chopped lettuce on each of six chilled salad plates. Cover each with ½ cup hearts of palm and garnish with two half slices of tomato. Chill.

Pour ¼ cup Vinaigrette Sauce over each salad and serve.

Serves 6.

SALADE AUX POINTES D'ASPERGES
Asparagus Tip Salad

½ cup chopped lettuce leaves	1 slice tomato, halved
6 cooked asparagus tips, cold	¼ cup Vinaigrette Sauce, page 117

Cover a chilled salad plate with ½ cup chopped lettuce leaves. Lay the asparagus tips over the lettuce and garnish the plate with 2 halves of a sliced tomato. Cover with ¼ cup Vinaigrette Sauce and serve.

Serves 1.

DESSERTS
Desserts

Gus Guerra, at Antoine's for 10 years, worked in the dining room before he became the kitchen steward. The beautiful Omelette Alaska Antoine (Baked Alaska) is a house specialty.

The end of the meal and the finishing touch. As simple as Creme Caramel or as glamorous as Omelette Alaska Antoine, the dessert becomes the final brushstrokes of a masterpiece in fine dining.

CREME GLACEE AUX FRAISES
Ice Cream with Strawberries

½ cup fresh strawberries
½ cup vanilla ice cream

Wash and hull the strawberries. Scoop out the ice cream into a bowl and top with the strawberries.

Serves 1.

FRAISES AU KIRSCH
Strawberries with Kirsch

¾ cup strawberries
⅓ cup kirsch
1 tablespoon sugar

Wash and hull the strawberries. Put them in a dessert dish and chill. To serve, pour the kirsch over the strawberries and sprinkle with one tablespoon sugar.

Serves 1.

MERINGUE GLACEE SAUCE CHOCOLAT
Baked Meringue Shell with Ice Cream and Chocolate Sauce

1 baked meringue shell
1 large scoop vanilla ice cream
⅓ cup hot fudge topping

Top the meringue shell with a large scoop of vanilla ice cream. Cover the ice cream with ⅓ cup hot fudge topping.

Serves 1.

MOUSSE AU CHOCOLAT
Chocolate Mousse

⅔ cup dark semi-sweet
   chocolate chips
¼ teaspoon salt
2 tablespoons water

4 eggs, separated
1 teaspoon vanilla extract
¾ cup whipping cream
1 teaspoon sugar

Put the chocolate chips, salt and water together in a saucepan and place on a low heat until the chocolate is melted. Remove from the heat and mix the egg yolks and vanilla extract into the chocolate.

Whip up ½ cup of the whipping cream and fold this into the chocolate mixture. Now whip the four egg whites until they form stiff peaks, and fold this also into the mixture. Spoon into six cups and chill.

To serve, whip up the remaining ¼ cup whipping cream with a teaspoon of sugar and top each mousse with a spoon of the sweetened whipped cream.

Serves 6.

OMELETTE ALASKA ANTOINE
Baked Alaska

1 pound cake
7 large egg whites
¼ teaspoon salt

¾ cup and 3 tablespoons fine
granulated sugar
1 quart vanilla ice cream

Slice the pound cake into ¾ inch slices and set aside. Whip up the egg whites with the salt until they are foamy and can hold their shape. Gradually add ¾ cup of the sugar as you continue whipping, until the egg whites become shiny and stand in stiff peaks.

Line the bottom of a 12 to 14 inch oval pan with some of the cake slices. Scoop the ice cream onto the cake slices in an oval shape. Put the rest of the cake slices around the sides and top of the ice cream.

Cover the ice cream and cake with the whipped whites, using all but one cup. Smooth out the egg whites with a spatula. Whip the remaining egg whites with 3 tablespoons of sugar and put into a pastry bag fitted with a small nozzle.

Brown the Alaska quickly under a broiler flame or in a hot preheated 450°F oven for 4 minutes. Decorate with the remaining egg white and serve, using 2 large spoons to scoop out each portion.

Serves 6.

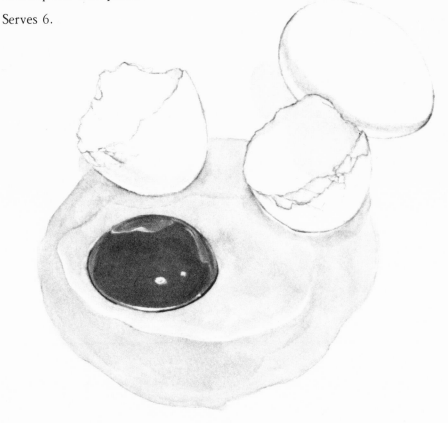

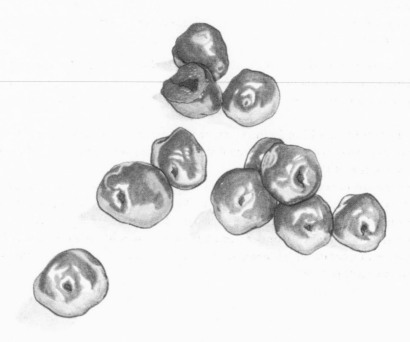

CERISES JUBILEE
Cherries Jubilee

1 quart vanilla ice cream
3 cups canned bing cherries
2 cups brandy

Scoop the ice cream out into six dessert dishes. Put the cherries and brandy into a metal mixing bowl and heat over a flame until the brandy is hot but not boiling. Ignite the brandy with a match and mix the cherries, while flaming, for a brief moment in the bowl.

Spoon the cherries and brandy (still flaming) over the ice cream and serve.

Serves 6.

PECHE MELBA
Peach Melba

The great French chef Auguste Escoffier created this dish in 1893 for the celebrated Australian singer Nelly Melba.

PEACH MELBA

6 slices pound cake
3 cups vanilla ice cream
6 peach halves

1 cup grenadine syrup
⅔ cup chopped roasted almonds

Place a slice of pound cake in the bottom of each of six dessert bowls. Top each with a scoop of vanilla ice cream (about ½ cup) and then a peach half, cut side down, on the ice cream. Pour over some grenadine syrup and sprinkle with chopped, roasted almonds.

Serves 6.

CREPES SUZETTE
French Pancakes Suzette

This dish was created for the Prince of Wales, the future Edward VII, in 1898, at the Cafe de Paris in Monte Carlo. The prince himself named it after his lovely compagne, Suzette.

CREPE BATTER

¾ cup flour
1 teaspoon sugar
½ teaspoon salt

2 whole eggs
1½ cups milk, scalded
1½ tablespoons butter

Sift the flour into a mixing bowl, add the salt, two whole eggs, and half the milk. Whisk thoroughly, add the remaining milk, and whisk some more. Let it rest.

Just before making the crepes, melt 1½ tablespoons butter and whisk into the batter.

PREPARATION OF CREPES

1 stick butter
crepe batter

Melt butter in a small pan to use in coating the crepe pan. The crepe pan should have a base of about 6 inches.

Heat the bottom and sides of the crepe pan very well, then spoon some melted butter into the pan to coat the bottom and sides. Pour the excess butter back into the butter pan. Pour three tablespoons batter into the pan. Tilt the pan from side to side to completely coat the bottom. Use a knife blade to push down any batter which may cling to the sides of the pan. When the batter in the pan all becomes dry, flip the crepe and cook for about 30 seconds on the other side.

Place the cooked crepes one on the other on a dish and cover with a damp cloth.

Makes about 15 crepes.

FILLING

½ cup powdered sugar
2 tablespoons grated orange rind
1 tablespoon vanilla
2 tablespoons orange juice

1 tablespoon lemon juice
2 tablespoons brandy
2 tablespoons melted butter

Combine all ingredients and keep at room temperature.

LIQUEURS FOR BURNING

5 ounces Orange Curacao   3 ounces maraschino liqueur
3 ounces Triple Sec   3 ounces kirsch

Combine all liqueurs.

TO SERVE

Spread each crepe, using 2 per person, with 1 tablespoon of the filling and roll up. Place the twelve crepes in a chafing dish and pour in the liqueur mixture. Heat over a flame until hot, and ignite with a match. Spoon the flaming liqueurs over the crepes until the fire goes out. Serve 2 crepes per person with some of the liqueurs poured over.

Serves 6.

ORANGE BRULOT
Burning Orange

1 orange
1 sugar cube
2 ounces brandy

Put the orange in a pot and cover with boiling water. Soak the orange in the hot water for 5 minutes. Remove the orange from the water and while it is still warm make a skin-deep cut around the center of the orange. Now carefully fold the skin back on the orange, top and bottom, to form cups.

To serve, stand the orange on one cup and put a sugar cube in the top cup. Fill the cup with warmed brandy and ignite. When the brandy has stopped burning it should be sipped with a spoon.

Serves 1.

CREME RENVERSEE AU CARAMEL
Caramel Custard

1 cup sugar
1 tablespoon water
4 whole eggs
2 egg yolks

3 cups half and half
1 teaspoon vanilla extract
¼ teaspoon salt

Put ½ cup of the sugar in a small saucepan with 1 tablespoon water and heat until the sugar has become a light-brown caramelized syrup. Pour this syrup immediately into the bottom of six custard cups.

In a mixing bowl combine the whole eggs, the yolks, ½ cup sugar, vanilla and salt. Heat the half and half until just below boiling and slowly pour into the egg mixture, mixing constantly to avoid cooking the eggs. Pour this mixture into the six custard cups and put them in a pan filled with hot water. Place the pan in a preheated low 325 °F oven for about one hour or until a knife inserted into the center of the custard comes out clean. Remove from the oven and chill in the refrigerator.

To serve, remove the custards from the refrigerator and loosen the edges with a sharp knife. Turn out onto chilled dessert plates.

Serves 6.

Antoine's has one of the largest wine cellars in America, with a stock of over 25,000 bottles. Beverage manager Don Fonseca also directs the preparation of Antoine's special drinks (in the city where the cocktail was invented).

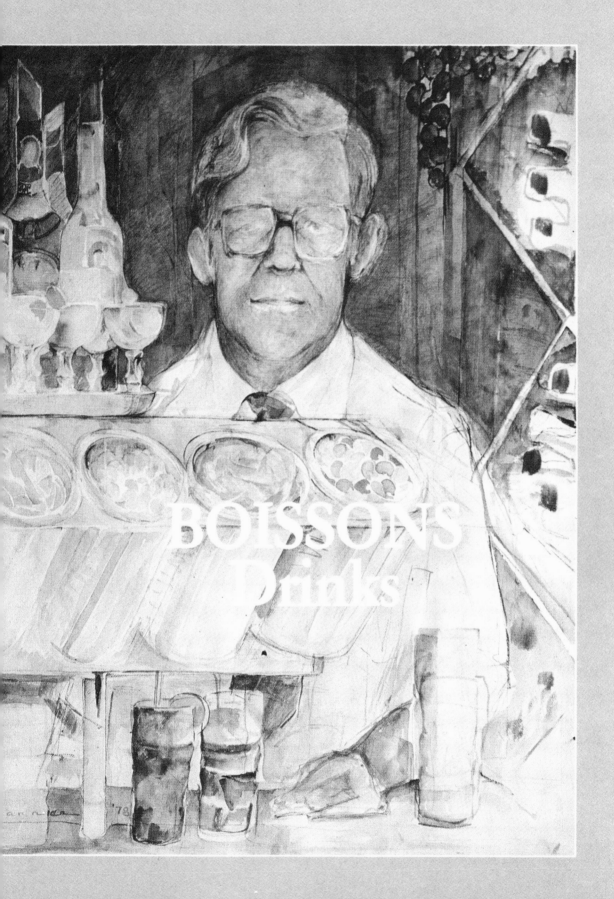

BOISSONS
Drinks

As we have our own cuisine, we also have our own drinks. We have drinks for any time of the day, morning, afternoon, or evening. The following recipes are for those that are most popular.

AMBROSIA

¾ ounce brandy
¾ ounce Cointreau
4 ounces chilled champagne

Shake the brandy and Cointreau together with ice and strain into a champagne glass. Add the champagne.

ANTOINE'S PORTO SHAKE

1 ounce port wine
1 ounce brandy
1 ounce orange juice

1 ounce pineapple juice
1 teaspoon triple sec
1 teaspoon anisette

Shake ingredients with crushed ice and pour into a highball glass. Add more crushed ice and serve with straws.

ANTOINE'S SMILE

1½ ounces calvados
½ ounce lemon juice

½ ounce simple syrup
dash grenadine

Shake with ice and strain into a martini glass.

BACCHUS COCKTAIL

1½ ounces Dubonnet
1½ ounces dry vermouth
lemon twist

Pour the ingredients over ice into a cocktail glass. Stir. Add a lemon twist.

BLOODY MARY

1½ ounces vodka
5 ounces tomato juice
½ ounce lemon juice

dash worcestershire
dash Tabasco Sauce
¾ cup crushed ice

Combine ingredients in an electric blender with ¾ cup crushed ice and serve in a large wine glass.

FRENCH 75

1½ ounces gin
1 ounce lemon juice

1 ounce simple syrup
champagne

Pour the first three ingredients over ice in a highball glass and stir. Fill with champagne.

JUBILEE COCKTAIL

¾ ounce gin
¾ ounce triple sec
½ ounce lemon juice

½ ounce simple syrup
few drops green food coloring

Shake all ingredients together with ice and strain into a martini glass.

MILK PUNCH

1½ ounces brandy or bourbon
1 ounce simple syrup
½ teaspoon orange flower water

½ teaspoon vanilla extract
4 ounces light cream
grated nutmeg

Mix the first five ingredients together in an electric blender with ½ cup crushed ice. Pour into a highball glass and top with grated nutmeg.

MINT JULEP

4 mint leaves
1 tablespoon sugar

1½ ounces bourbon whiskey
1 sprig mint

Use a mortar and pestle to crush the mint leaves with the sugar into a paste. Put the mint paste and the bourbon in a highball glass and fill with crushed ice. Stir until the glass frosts on the outside. Serve garnished with a sprig of mint and straws.

ORANGE BLOSSOM

1½ ounces gin
1 ounce simple syrup

3 ounces orange juice
1 teaspoon orange flower water

Shake all ingredients together with ice and strain into a martini glass.

RAMOS GIN FIZZ

1½ ounces gin
1 teaspoon powdered sugar
½ teaspoon orange flower water
½ teaspoon vanilla extract

1 egg white
3 ounces light cream
soda

Mix with ½ cup crushed ice in a blender. Pour into a highball glass and fill with soda.

RUSTY NAIL

1 ounce scotch whiskey
½ ounce Drambuie

Pour ingredients over ice in a cocktail glass. Stir.

SAZERAC

1½ ounces rye whiskey
½ ounce simple syrup
1 dash Peychaud's Bitters

1 tablespoon Herbsaint (a New
      Orleans made Pernod-type liquor)
lemon twist

Shake the first four ingredients together with ice and strain into a cocktail glass. Add a lemon twist.

SCARLET O'HARA

1½ ounces Southern Comfort
1 ounce lime juice
3 ounces cranberry juice

Shake with ice and strain into a champagne glass.

SHERRY FLIP

3 ounces cream sherry
1 ounce simple syrup
1 raw egg

½ teaspoon vanilla extract
grated nutmeg

Mix the ingredients in an electric blender with ½ cup crushed ice. Pour into a large wine glass and top with grated nutmeg.

VELVET HAMMER

¾ ounce Cointreau
¾ ounce brandy
1 ounce light cream

Shake the ingredients together with ice and strain into a martini glass.

CAFE BRULOT DIABOLIQUE

2 sticks cinnamon
8 whole cloves
peel of one lemon

1½ tablespoons sugar
3 ounces brandy
3 cups strong black coffee, hot

Put the cinnamon, cloves, lemon peel, sugar and brandy in a fireproof bowl and heat on an open flame. When the brandy is hot, but not boiling, bring the bowl to the table and ignite with a match. Use a ladle to stir and pour the liquid around in the bowl for 2 minutes. Pour the hot coffee into the flaming brandy and then ladle into demitasse cups (half cups).

At Antoine's we use a special copper Brulot Bowl and special cups which were designed by my great-grandfather Jules Alciatore.

Serves 6.

INDEX